The Original

BOOK OF BOB

Volume 1

By

Robert "BOB" John Keiber

Given to: ______________________ From: ______________________

Date: ______________________ Occasion: ______________________

Author's Assistant

Jennifer Bocanegra

Belle Chan

Edited By

Ellen Thomas

Dedicated to

Theodora "Teddy" Keiber

Declan Robert "Bob" Keiber

&

Over 8 million Bobs in America

Published by

The Tuxedo Group

Suite 2514

244 5th Avenue

New York City 10001

thetuxedogroup@yahoo.com

Facebook @ The Book of Bob

Websites ;

bookofbob.info

bookof bob.club

Volume 1

Table of Contents

Introduction

Why We Need This Book

If you are reading this book you most likely are named Bob, or you may know someone named Bob, and everybody knows someone named Bob. In either case you may or may not be aware that the name Bob has an identity crisis. What is a Bob, Who is a Bob and Why is a Bob? Why are there so many Bobs in TV and Radio commercials, on greeting cards and in the movies?

If those questions constantly nag at you, then keep on reading because this book is for you. If these questions don't bother you at all, read it anyway, or go find a book named Walter. Don't bother you, won't find one.

The very first problem with the name Bob is that it is spelled the same way backwards and forwards.(If you have to write the name out in pencil and hold it to a mirror to prove this, you shouldn't be walking around with sharp things like pencils in the first place. Bob is a palindrome. What's a palindrome? It's in this book! How lucky are you?

In any case, the fact that Bob is a palindrome (hint; So is Eve. Don't tell Adam.) means Bob is totally reversible, and that should tell you something. I don't know what. But I do believe that this fact alone is the very reason why there has never been a pope named Bob, or for that matter why there is no Bob in the Bible, although as you may or may not remember there is an Eve. But in all fairness consider the possible passage "Bob, build me an ark!" Not the same impact and it would take some getting used to.

Granted, it may be a little too late to add The Book of Bob to the Bible. That ark has already sailed. Not that the Book of Job would be missed if Bob replaced it. Let's be honest, the Book of Job may have some very valuable lessons in patience, but all and all, that book is downright depressing. I doubt if Bob would have been that understanding. I submit that the book of Bob has some lessons too, few of which might even be worth learning. You decide that after the read the book. That is why you need this book. I thought it was appropriate to say that here, just to keep you hooked.

For those of you who actually do read English, you will be excited to know that not only is the name Bob reversible, but on top of that it is both a noun and a verb. You might say it is bi-grammatical. Some people are even trying to make it an adjective: They go around saying; "That's very Bob of you." but it's not really catching on. In fact this last part is really not true. I made it up to try and start a trend. However, in England Bob is almost an adjective. They use a phrase, "Bob's your uncle." which has nothing to do with long lost relatives. What this vague statement means is "and there it is, or that's it." as in the act of giving directions to the nearest pub. Let me give you an example of such directions. "You go down one block, turn to your right, and Bob's your uncle!" I have no idea why the English came up with that ridiculous phrase, but they always did have a problem with the English language.

If you're from a foreign country and don't speak English and wondering how to pronounce Bob and what Bob means, I'm wondering why you're even trying to read this book in the first place. If you can't find an interpreter, get an English dictionary.

The dictionary offers this under bob, Bob;

Pronunciation: (bob), [key]- n., v., bobbed, bobbing

1. noun;. A tap; light blow,

2. A polishing wheel of leather

1-verb..-To tap, strike lightly.

2, to move up and down

At this point it becomes apparent that the word/name Bob comes from a striking motion, but a light one at that. This could be one of the reasons why the name Bob does not strike terror in the hearts of men, "Oh no, Bob's coming." "Whoopee do. I'm shaking." The name Bob, while not very scary, is not worthless. In fact in Britain it is the informal name for a shilling. While that's not the largest denomination in the realm and you need at least two Bobs to buy anything, it's worth more than two Jims any day. In fact nowhere in the world can you buy anything for two Jims. Why? Because as they say in marry old England, "two Bobs are better than one."

So the name Bob, if anything, is very flexible. Some usages are not as flattering as others Bob: a short jerky motion "a bob of the head." Now if you get Bob to bob Bob's head is that redundant, or do you just get a headache?

Of course an English Bobbie named Bob could bob the whole body, along with bobbing his head as he goes bobbing down the street. Then he really looks "jerky". If this particular Bob jumps into the ocean Bob could bob in the waves by moving about unexpectedly; such as in "a surprisingly familiar face bobbed up in the crowd. It was Bob." So Bob is not only flexible, but jerky and even surprising from time to time. That pretty much clarifies why there has never been a pope name Bob. Nobody wants a surprisingly jerky pope, even if he is flexible.

So, "Bob's your uncle!" (Remember, "thats it.") Now to answer my original question (Why We Need This Book) it's because if your name is Bob, you need to know everything you possibly can about Bob. If you know a Bob you need to do everything you can to support him in his quest for his true identity. More importantly you must help and support this Bob who wrote the book because I need the money, and you need a gift for Bob. Was that the longest introduction you have ever read, or what? Did I mention we have had three hurricanes named Bob? But wait there's more.

Chapter 1

In the Beginning there was Bob

Chapter 1-The Origin of Bob

What is a "Bob" and where did Bob come from?

Are these questions plaguing you? Me neither.

However, I have a book to write and you have a book to read.

Here are some other definitions that further confuse the issue:

BOB-*Pronunciation*; (bob), {key}

1. A style of short haircut for women and children. (Apparently Bob shouldn't get a bob)
2. A docked horse's tail. (Not to be confused with a horse's ass)
3. A dangling or swinging object, (get your mind out of the gutter) such as a weight on a pendulum or plumb line.
4. A short simple line in a verse or song, a short refrain or coda. (Sing a little bob for me)
5. A knot of worms, rages, etc. on a string. (very flattering)
6. A float for a fishing line. (What do you call a man with no arms and no legs floating in the ocean? A Bob.) I'm sorry.
7. A bob sled or bob skate.
8. A bunch, cluster, or wad, (in Scotland.)
9. To have your nose surgically turn up at the end.

   By now you have more information from the dictionary about a Bob than you ever dreamed necessary, or will ever need or use.

   With that in mind I'm going to give you more from the unofficial dictionary of Bob;

10. A bob-tail
11. A bob cat
12. bob-a-loo- (ask your mother about Ricky Ricardo. Fine, try your grandmother.)
13. Battery Operated Buddy. (A woman's vibrator) ("He's just my Bob.")
14. A bobby pin
15. Bobbed wire
16. Lorraina Bobbit (ouch)
17. Bobsy twins
18. A bobwhite (it's a bird)
19. Bob-ka (it's a bread)
20. Sponge Bob (I don't want to know)
21. Bobby socks
22. Bobbie-English Policeman (Who may or may not be named Bob)

Chapter 1-The Origin of Bob

There you have it. Bob's Your Uncle! Cheerio! What is my point?

My point is that Bob has an identity crisis and the name Bob is losing ground in popularity. During the years 1930-1939, Bob was number 85 of the most popular 1,000 names in the United States, only to slip to 578 in 1970. Of course that was during the hippie generation when everybody was naming their children Acme and Moonlint. After a couple of decades people finally got sober and started making sense. Bob did make a comeback in 1990 moving into 265 of the 1,000 most popular names. This most likely happened because when a lot of Acmes and Moonlints finally reached twenty-one, they snuck out of the house while their parents were having Purple Haze flashbacks, and legally changed their stupid names to something human like Bob. Aren't you glad they made that decision? Back in the 80s a lot of people were actually taking about doing away with Bob altogether. Well, not exactly a lot people, just my parents. But imagine if you will, a world without Bob. You would have to say, "Oh, there goes Frank, "Jimmying" down the street," or "Oh, be careful of that Bill-cat in the tree! I didn't know they climbed trees." The point here is you can't just do away with Bob. (Are you listening mom and dad?) The world would be a sadder place if you did. I'm sure you would agree.

At this point you are asking, why did I pick up this book? You picked it up because you wanted to know from where the name Bob originated. Excellent question! Bob is of English origin. That's why it's easy to pronounce if you speak English. Bob is the nickname for Robert. And don't forget the there is the popular greeting, "my name is Robert, but you can call me Bob."

Many people even like to interchange the name with Boob when addressing Bob. Well, not many people, just those in my family. I warn you, however, using Boob is a very bad idea when addressing a Bob, and never should it be used when addressing actor Bob (Robert) Blake. In fact it would be best never to address Robert Blake under any circumstances. Don't even make eye contact. Other famous Bob (Robert) luminaries would be Bob Hope, Robert (we close friends call him Bobby) DiNiro, and Bob (never call him Bobby) Dylan, More about them later in the book. Did I mention Bob Barker, the game show host?

Robert, being of English origin, was used for 3 characters by Shakespeare. Twelve saints carried the name and 25 Nobel Award winners were proud to bear it, as were 7 Oscar winners and a whole bunch of athletes. Three Kings of Scotland, who were actually named Raibert (close enough for rock and roll.) carried the tag, including Robert the Bruce. (Talk about split personality) The Normans introduced this name to Britain, although nobody is quite sure who introduced the name Norman to the Normans.

Chapter 1-The Origin of Bob

The name actually is very masculine and means “Bright Frame,” derived from the Germanic elements *hrod* “fame” and *beraht* “bright” (save that tidbit for networking events and watch them scatter.).

In English we pronounce it RAH-*burt* and:

Ro-BER-in French

Roberto- Italian, Spanish, Portuguese

Robi- Hungarian

Roibeard- Irish

Roope- Finnish

Rupert- German, Dutch, and Polish

And backwards it is pronounced Trebor, (Welsh) and means “One from a large villiage,” which, as far as I know, is not a very popular baby name.

But wait, there’s more.

Chapter 2

BOB is an Acronym

Chapter 2-Bob is an Acronym

This doesn't make him a bad person. What is an acronym? An acronym is a combination of letters that could be the initials of a variety of things, which have different meanings. For instance if your name is Bob and you drive around with a sign in the back of your car window that reads Bob On Board, people would most likely think you were a dork, as unfair as that might sound. However, many loving parents ride around with a sign in their back window, which reads Baby On Board. This sign allegedly makes other drivers proceed with caution when approaching such a car with its precious cargo. Good luck! To really keep some idiot drivers from tailgating you, you might do better with Bomb On Board. That acronym will cut you a wide path, my friend. That is until a state trooper spots you. Bob In Prison is not an acronym.

Do you have any more acronyms you can give us Bob? Absolutely.

Check these out.

BOB as a three-letter acronym could stand for:

- Band of Brothers, television series
- Bucket of Bolts, an old car
- Best of Breed, commonly used in reference to the computer industry or with dogs
- Blitter Object, a type of graphics construct available on the Commodore Amiga, later models of the Atari ST, and the Atari Lynx
- "The BOB" (Bank One Ballpark) is a nickname for Chase Field where the Arizona Diamondbacks baseball team plays
- B.O.B. (Bombs Over Baghdad), a 2000 single by OutKast
- Brains On Board, A personal robo concept designed by Androbot (a defunct company) in the 1980's
- "Born On Board" referring to many of the inhabitants of the UESC Marathon in the 1994 Marathon (computer game)
- Battery-Operated Boyfriend, a euphemism for a vibrator
- "Baby on Board," an automobile bumper sticker fad that was popular during the 1980s
- Bottom of the Basket, grocery slang for the lower part of a shopping cart, commonly use to remind clerks to check for additional items
- Back of Book (as in the software "BOB Advanced" which refers to cheating in math using the answers at the end of the book) BOB Advances Website (math equation solver)
- Back of the book (philately)
- Back of the book (publishing)
- Bank of Baroda

Chapter 2-Bob is an Acronym

- Bank Of Beirut- Not the safest place for your money
- Bank of Butterfield- Better
- Basketball Owl Band- Rice University's
- Battle Of Britain- Was your first wife English?
- Beast Of Burden- Did your first wife make a list of chores for you?
- Berner Oberland Bahn- A mountain railway in Switzerland
- Big Orange Ball- slang for the sun
- Boliviano (Bolivian currency)-keep it in the Bank of Beirut
- Bunch Of Believers, a Christian Ska group.
- B.O.B. (Branded Oak Bitter), a form of dark ale
  Bug-Out Bag- Keep it in the car. (Bag on Board)

Chapter 3

BOB is a Palindrome

Chapter 3- Bob is a Palindrome

The very first problem with the name BOB is that it is spelled the same way backwards and forwards.

If you have to write the name out in pencil and hold it to a mirror to prove this, you shouldn't be walking around with sharp things like pencils in the first place. Bob is a palindrome. That's right! I said it, and now it's out in the open. I want all you Bobs reading this, whoever you are, to shout out loud, "I'm a palindrome and I'm not going home!" I have no idea what that means. Ever try to rhyme something with palindrome. Before you go scrambling for a dictionary let me just tell you up front, palindrome is a word that can be spelled the same way backwards and forwards. Does it have the same meaning both ways? Of course! It's the same word. Don't wear me out with silly questions already, since you and I have a whole book to get though. You might ask, "What would be another palindrome?" How about "Kazak"? Yes, it's a real word. Kazak is a person who inhabits the central Asian republic of Kazakhstan. As you may remember this country is famous for having the largest population of wolves in the world. And all the time you thought Washington, DC had that title.

Do you want to know the longest palindrome in the Oxford English Dictionary? Sure you do. It is "TATTARRATTAT." Okay, I'll wait for you to get your pencil and mirror. No I won't. The word comes from James Joyce who coined it for his book Ulysses. You remember the book your mother wouldn't let you read and your father wouldn't give back to you? In any case the fact that Bob is totally reversible should tell you something. I don't know what. But, I do believe that this fact alone is the very reason why there has never been a pope named Bob, or for that matter why there is not Bob in the Bible. Consider the possible passage "Bob, build me an ark!" It would take some getting used to, I admit. Granted, it may be a little too late to add The Book of Bob to the Bible. That ark has already sailed. Not that the Book of Job would be missed if Bob replaced it. Let's be honest, the Book of Job may have some very valuable lessons in patience, but all and all, that book is downright depressing. I doubt if Bob would have been as understanding as Job. I submit that the Book of Bob has some lessons too- a few which might even be worth learning…but you decide. That is why you need this book. I thought it was appropriate to say that here, just to keep you hooked.

Are you hooked? Read on anyway.

Chapter 4

BOB in Television and Film

Chapter 4- Television and Film

What About Bob? (The Movie)

What About Bob? is a 1991 comedy film directed by Frank Oz, and starring Bill Murrayand Richard Dreyfuss. Murray plays Bob Wiley, a psychiatric patient who follows his egotistical psychiatrist Dr. Leo Marvin (Dreyfuss) on vacation. When the unstable Bob befriends the other members of Marvin's family, it pushes the doctor over the edge. This film is number 43 on Bravo's "100 Funniest Movies"

God, the Devil and Bob (TV series)

God, the Devil and Bob is an animated sitcom which premiered on NBC on March 9, 2000 and ended on March 28, 2000, leaving nine episodes unaired. It was not a very big hit.

Robert Altman (film director)

February 20, 1925 – November 20, 2006) was an American film director, screenwriter, and producer. A five time nominee of the Academy Award for Best Director and an enduring figure from the New Hollywood era, Altman was considered a "maverick" in making films that are highly naturalistic, but with a stylized perspective unlike most Hollywood films. He is consistently ranked as one of the greatest and most influential filmmakers in history.His style of filmmaking was unique among directors in that his subjects covered most genres but with a "subversive" twist, typically relying on satire and humor to express his personal vision. Altman developed a reputation for being "anti-Hollywood" and non-conformist in both his themes and directing style. However, actors especially enjoyed working under his direction because he encouraged them to improvise, thereby inspiring their own creativity.

Robert Alda (actor)

Robert Alda (February 26, 1914 – May 3, 1986) was an American theatrical and filmactor and father of actors Alan and Antony Alda. A talented singer and dancer, Alda was featured in a number of Broadway productions before moving to Italy during the early 1960s. He appeared in many European films over the next two decades, occasionally returning to the U.S. for film appearances such as The Girl Who Knew Too Much (1969).Alda, an American of Italian descent, was born Alphonso Giuseppe Giovanni Roberto D'Abruzzo in New York, New York, the son of Frances (née Tumillo) and Antonio D'Abruzzo, a barber born in Sant'Agata de' Goti, Benevento, Campania, Italy. He graduated from Stuyvesant High School in New York in 1930. He began as a singer anddancer in vaudeville after winning a talent contest, and moved on to burlesque.

Alda is known for portraying George Gershwin in the biopic Rhapsody in Blue (1945) as well as the talent agent in the Douglas Sirk classic Imitation of Life (1959). He was very successful on Broadway, starring in Guys and Dolls (1950), for which he won a Tony Award, and in What Makes Sammy Run? (1964). He was also the host of the short-lived DuMont TV version of the game show What's Your Bid? (May–June 1953).

Alda's first wife, and mother of actor Alan Alda, Joan Browne, was a homemaker and former beauty pageant winner. Alda was married to his second wife, Flora Marino, an Italian actress whom he met in Rome, until his death. Alda made two guest appearances with his son Alan Alda on M*A*S*H, in the episodes "The Consultant" (January 1975) and "Lend a Hand" (February 1980). The latter episode also featured Antony Alda (1956–2009), his younger son by his second wife. Alda died on May 3, 1986, aged 72, after a long illness following a stroke.

"Baghdad Bob" Muhammad Saeed al-Sahhaf (spokesperson for IRAQ)

Muḥammad Saʿīd Al-Ṣaḥḥāf; born 1940) is a former Iraqi diplomat and politician. He came to wide prominence around the world during the 2003 invasion of Iraq, during which he was the Iraqi Information Minister under Iraqi president Saddam Hussein, acting as the spokesperson for the Arab Socialist Ba'ath Party and Saddam's regime.

He is best known for his grandiose and grossly unrealistic propaganda broadcasts before and during the war, extolling the invincibility of the Iraqi Army and the permanence of Saddam's rule. His announcements were intended for an Iraqi domestic audience subject to Saddam's cult of personality and total state censorship, and were met with widespread derision and amusement by Western nationals and others with access to up-to-date information from international media organizations. In the US he was popularly known asBaghdad Bob, in the UK as Comical Ali, and in Italy as Alì il Comico

Robert William "Bob" Barker (game show host)
Born December 12, 1923, he is an American former television game show host. He is best known for hosting CBS's The Price Is Right from 1972 to 2007, making it the longest-running daytime game show in North American television history, and for hosting Truth or Consequences from 1956 to 1974.

Born in Washington State to modest circumstances, Barker enlisted in the United States Navyon the outbreak of World War II. Barker worked part-time in radio while he attended college. In 1950, Barker moved to California in order to pursue a career in broadcasting. He was given his own radio show, The Bob Barker Show, which ran for the next six years from Burbank.

Barker began his game show career in 1956, hosting Truth or Consequences. From there, he hosted various game shows as well as the Miss Universe pageants. Eventually, he hosted The Price Is Right, beginning in 1972. When his wife Dorothy Jo died, Barker became an advocate for animal rights. Since then, Barker has been a long-time supporter of animal rights, and of animal-rights activism, including groups such as the United Activists for Animal Rights and the Sea Shepherd Conservation Society. In 2007, Barker retired from hosting The Price Is Right after celebrating his 50-year career on television.

Robert Blake (actor)

Robert Blake (born September 18, 1933) is an American actor having starring roles in the film In Cold Blood and the U.S. television series Baretta. Blake began performing as a child, with a lead role in the final years of MGM's Our Gang(Little Rascals) short film series from 1939 to 1944. He also appeared as a child actor in 22 entries of the Red Ryder film franchise. In the Red Ryder series and in many of his other roles as an adult, he was cast as a Native American or Latino character.

After a stint in the army, Blake returned to acting in both television and movie roles. He was married to Sondra Kerr, his first wife with whom he had two children, from 1964 until their divorce in 1983. He continued acting through 1997's Lost Highway for a career that author Michael Newton called "one of the longest in Hollywood history."

In 2005, Blake was tried and acquitted of the 2001 murder of his second wife, Bonnie Lee Bakley, but on November 18, 2005, Blake was found liable in a California civil court for her wrongful death.

Bob's Burgers (TV cartoon series)

Bob's Burgers is an American animated sitcom created by Loren Bouchardfor the Fox Broadcasting Company. The series centers on the Belchers—parents Bob and Linda, and their children Tina, Gene, and Louise—who run ahamburger restaurant. The family was conceived by Bouchard after he developed *Home Movies*.
Since its debut on January 9, 2011, the series has broadcast 88 episodes. While reviews for the first season were mixed, feedback for subsequent seasons has been very positive.

Chapter 4- Television and Film

Bob Denver (actor)

Robert Osbourne "Bob" Denver (January 9, 1935 – September 2, 2005) was an American comedic actor known for his roles as Gilligan on the television series *Gilligan's Island* and the beatnik Maynard G. Krebs on the 1959–1963 TV series The Many Loves of Dobie Gillis.

Denver was born in New Rochelle, New York, and raised in Brownwood, Texas. He graduated from Loyola University in Los Angeles, California. He later coached physical education and taught mathematics and history at Corpus Christi School, a Roman Catholic elementary school in Pacific Palisades, California.

While teaching at Corpus Christi in 1958, Denver shot the pilot for the TV series The Many *Loves of Dobie Gillis*, and left teaching for his first professional acting job as a regular on the series when it was picked up in 1959. From 1959 to 1963, Denver appeared on Dobie Gillis as Maynard G. Krebs, the teenaged beatnik best friend of Dobie Gillis, played by Dwayne Hickman. While he was on Dobie Gillis, Denver also appeared on the NBC interview program, *Here's Hollywood.*

Robert Evans (film producer)

Robert Evans (born June 29, 1930) is an American film producer and former studio executive, best known for his work on Rosemary's Baby, Love Story, The Godfather andChinatown. Evans was born Robert J. Shapera in New York City, New York, the son of Florence, a housewife who came from a wealthy family, and Archie Shapera, a dentist in Harlem. He has described both of his parents as "second-generation Jews." He grew up on New York City's Upper West Side during the 1930s, where he was better off than most people living during the Great Depression. In his early years, he did promotional work for Evan-Picone, a fashion company founded by his brother Charles, in addition to doing voice work on radio shows.

He was spotted by actress Norma Shearer next to the pool at The Beverly Hills Hotel on Election Day, 1956. She successfully touted him for the role of her late husband Irving Thalberg in Man of a Thousand Faces. The same year, Evans also caught the eye of Darryl F. Zanuck, who cast him as Pedro Romero in the 1957 film adaptation of Ernest Hemingway's The Sun Also Rises, against the wishes of co-star Ava Gardner and Hemingway himself. In 1959, he appeared in Twentieth Century Fox's production of The Best of Everything with Hope Lange, Diane Baker andJoan Crawford.

Chapter 4- Television and Film

Bob and Ray (comedy duo)

Ray Goulding and Bob Elliott hosting The Name's the Samein 1955. For the real-life Tex Blaisdell, see Tex Blaisdell. Bob and Ray was an American comedy duo whose career spanned five decades. Composed of comedians Bob Elliott (born 1923) and Ray Goulding (1922–1990), the duo's format was typically to satirize the medium in which they were performing, such as conducting radio ortelevision interviews, with off-the-wall dialogue presented in a generallydeadpan style as though it were a serious broadcast.

Bob Crane (actor)

Robert Edward "Bob" Crane (July 13, 1928 – June 29, 1978) was an American actor, drummer, radio host, and disc jockey. Crane began his career as a disc jockey in New York and Connecticut before moving toLos Angeles where he hosted the number-one rated morning show. In the early 1960s, he moved into acting. Crane is best known for his performance as Colonel Robert E. Hogan in the CBS sitcom Hogan's Heroes. The series aired from 1965 to 1971, and Crane received two Primetime Emmy Award nominations for his work on the series.

After Hogan's Heroes ended, Crane's career declined. He became frustrated with the few roles he was being offered and began doing dinner theater. In 1975, he returned to television in the NBC series The Bob Crane Show. The series received poor ratings and was cancelled after 13 weeks. Afterwards, Crane returned to performing in dinner theaters and also appeared in occasional guest spots on television. While on tour for his play Beginner's Luck in June 1978, Crane was found bludgeoned to death in his Scottsdale apartment, a murder that remains officially unsolved.

Robert Culp (actor)

Robert Martin Culp (August 16, 1930 – March 24, 2010) was an American actor, screenwriter, voice actor and director, widely known for his work in television. Culp earned an international reputation for his role as Kelly Robinson on I Spy (1965–1968), the espionage series in which he and co-star Bill Cosby played a pair of secret agents. Prior to that, he starred in the CBS/Four Star western series, Trackdown as Texas Ranger Hoby Gilman from 1957-1959. The 1980s brought him back to television. He starred as FBI Agent Bill Maxwell on The Greatest American Hero and also had a recurring role as Warren Whelan on *Everybody Loves Raymond.* In all, Culp gave hundreds of performances in a career spanning more than 50 years.

Chapter 4- Television and Film

Robert Cummings (actor)

Charles Clarence Robert Orville Cummings (June 9, 1910 – December 2, 1990) was an American film and television actor known mainly for his roles in comedy films such asThe Devil and Miss Jones (1941) and Princess O'Rourke (1943), but was also effective in dramatic films, especially two of Alfred Hitchcock's thrillers, Saboteur (1942) and Dial M for Murder (1954). Cummings received five Primetime Emmy Award nominations, and won the Primetime Emmy Award for Best Actor in a Single Performance in 1955. In 1960, he received two stars on the Hollywood Walk of Fame for motion pictures and television.

Robert Conrad

Bob Conrad (born March 1, 1935) is an American film and television actor, best known for his role in the 1965–1969 CBS television series *The Wild Wild West*, playing the sophisticated Secret Service agent James T. West. He also portrayed World War II ace Pappy Boyington in the television series *Black Sheep Squadron*. He was a recording artist of pop/rock songs in the early 1960s as **Bob Conrad** before he began his acting career. He has hosted a weekly two hour national radio show (*The PM Show with Robert Conrad*) on CRN Digital Talk Radio since 20 years old.

Robert De Niro (actor)

Robert De Niro (/də'nɪroʊ/; born August 17, 1943) is an American actor and film producer who has starred in over 90 films. His first major film roles were in the sports drama Bang the Drum Slowly (1973) and the Martin Scorsese-directed crime film Mean Streets (1973). In 1974, after being turned down for the role of Sonny Corleone in the crime filmThe Godfather (1972), he was cast as the young Vito Corleone in The Godfather Part II (1974), a role for which he won the Academy Award for Best Supporting Actor.

He received additional Academy Award nominations for Michael Cimino's Vietnam war drama The Deer Hunter (1978), Penny Marshall's drama Awakenings (1990), and David O. Russell's romantic comedy-drama Silver Linings Playbook (2012). His portrayal of gangster Jimmy Conway in Scorsese's crime film Goodfellas (1990) earned him a BAFTAnomination in 1990.

Chapter 4- Television and Film

Robert Downey Jr. (actor)

Robert John Downey Jr. (born April 4, 1965) is an American actor, producer, and singer, whose career has included critical and popular success in his youth, followed by a period of substance abuse and legal troubles, and a resurgence of commercial success in middle age.

Making his screen debut at the age of five, appearing in his father Robert Downey Sr.'s film Pound (1970), he appeared in roles associated with the Brat Pack, such as the teen sci-fi comedy Weird Science (1985) and the drama Less Than Zero (1987). Other films he has starred in include the action comedy Air America (1990), the comedy Soapdish (1991), and the crime film Natural Born Killers (1994). He starred as Charlie Chaplin, the title character in the 1992 film Chaplin, which earned him a nomination for the Academy Award for Best Actor.

After being released in 2000 from the California Substance Abuse Treatment Facility and State Prison where he was on drug charges, Downey joined the cast of the TV series Ally McBeal playing Calista Flockhart's love interest. His performance was praised and he received a Golden Globe Award for Best Performance by an Actor in a Supporting Role in a Series, Miniseries, or Television Film. His character was written out when Downey was fired after two drug arrests in late 2000 and early 2001. After one last stay in a court-ordered drug treatment program, Downey finally achieved sobriety.

Downey has starred in six movies that have each grossed over $500 million at the box office worldwide. Two of those films, The Avengers and Iron Man 3, each earned over $1 billion. Downey tops the Forbes list of Hollywood's highest-paid actors with an estimated $75 million in earnings between June 2012 and June 2013. Chapter 4- Television and Film

Jim Bob Duggar (reality television star)

James Robert "Jim Bob" Duggar (born July 18, 1965) is an American real estate agent, politician, and television personality on the now suspended reality series 19 Kids and Counting due to a sex scandal. He served in the Arkansas House of Representatives (1999-2002).

Chapter 4- Television and Film

Bobcat Goldthwait (comedian, actor)

Robert Francis "Bobcat" Goldthwait (born May 26, 1962) is an American film director, stand-up comedian, actor, writer, singer, voice artist, and comedian, known for his acerbic black comedy, delivered through an energetic stage personality with an unusual gruff and high-pitched voice.

Goldthwait was born Robert Francis Goldthwait in Syracuse, New York on May 26, 1962, the son of Tom Goldthwait, a sheet metal worker, and Kathleen, a department store employee. He was raised in a Catholic working-class family. At an early age, Goldthwait decided on a career as a comedian and was performing professionally while still in high school at age 15. He attended St. Matthew's grammar school in East Syracuse, New York, where he met Tom Kenny in 1st grade. In 1980, they graduated together from Bishop Grimes Junior/Senior High School in East Syracuse, New York. They formed a comedy troupe with Tom Nettle called the Generic Comics. Although nicknamed "Bobcat" and "Tomcat," they did not appear as a comedy team together. Early in his career, Goldthwait also co-wrote with Martin Olson, who is listed as writer on his first two comedy specials Share the Warmth and Don't Watch This Show.

Bob Hoskins (actor)

Robert William "Bob" Hoskins (26 October 1942 – 29 April 2014) was an English actor, known for playing Cockneys and gangsters. His best known works include lead roles inThe Long Good Friday (1980), Mona Lisa (1986), Who Framed Roger Rabbit (1988),Mermaids (1990), Super Mario Bros. (1993), and supporting performances in Brazil(1985), Hook (1991), Nixon (1995), Mrs. Henderson Presents (2005), A Christmas Carol(2009), Made in Dagenham (2010), and Snow White and the Huntsman (2012).

Hoskins received the prestigious Prix d'interprétation masculine, and won the BAFTA Award for Best Actor in a Leading Role and the Golden Globe Award for Best Actor – Motion Picture Drama for his role in Mona Lisa. He was also nominated for the Academy Award for Best Actor for the same role. In 2009, he won an International Emmy Award for Best Actor for his appearance on the BBC One drama The Street.

Chapter 4- Television and Film

Bobby Hill (King of the Hill cartoon character)

Robert Jeffrey "Bobby" Hill (born January 6, 1986) is a character on the animated series King of the Hill and is voiced by Pamela Adlon. Bobby is the only child of Hank andPeggy Hill. His middle name is named after his mom's dad and he has more characteristics to his mother, Peggy Hill, which is stated in the episode Square Peg.

Bob Hope (comedian, actor)

Leslie Townes "Bob" Hope, (May 29, 1903 – July 27, 2003), was an English-born American comedian, vaudevillian, actor, singer, dancer, athlete, and author. With a career spanning nearly 80 years, Hope appeared in over 70 films and shorts, including a series of "Road" movies co-starring Bing Crosby and Dorothy Lamour. In addition to hosting the Academy Awards fourteen times (more than any other host), he appeared in many stage productions and television roles and was the author of fourteen books. The song "Thanks For the Memory" is widely regarded as Hope's signature tune.
Celebrated for his long career performing United Service Organizations (USO) shows to entertain active service American military personnel—he made 57 tours for the USO between 1941 and 1991—Hope was declared an honorary veteran of the United States Armed Forces in 1997 by act of the U.S. Congress.

Hope participated in the sports of golf and boxing, and owned a small stake in his hometown baseball team, the Cleveland Indians. He was married to performer Dolores Hope (née DeFina) for 69 years. Hope died at age 100 at his home in Toluca Lake, California.

Bob Keeshan (actor)

Robert James "Bob" Keeshan (June 27, 1927 – January 23, 2004) was an American television producer and actor. He is most notable as the title character of the children's television program Captain Kangaroo, which became an icon for millions of people during its 30-year run from 1955 to 1984.

Keeshan also played the original "Clarabell the Clown" on the Howdy Doody television program. Keeshan was born in Lynbrook, New York. After an early graduation from Forest Hills High School in Queens, NY in 1945, during World War II, he enlisted in the United States Marine Corps Reserve, but was still in the United States when Japan surrendered. He attended Fordham University on the GI Bill and few years at Hillsdale College.

Chapter 4- Television and Film

Robert Klein (comedian, actor)

His first major appearance was as host of the 1970 summer replacement television series Comedy Tonight, on which were introduced many of the routines that in the next few years would be released on record albums. His extensive routines about the Watergate scandal made him highly popular in the 1970s. In 1974, he appeared in an episode of Paul Sand in Friends and Lovers.

Klein starred in HBO's first stand-up comedy special in 1975 during the cable channel's early broadcast days and has continued to appear in several more one-man shows which have typically concluded with his "I can't stop my leg" routine. In 1979, Klein was nominated for a Tony Award for Best Actor in a Musical for his role in They're Playing Our Song. In 1985, he starred in the "Wordplay" episode of The New Twilight Zone. In 1986, Klein had his own late night talk show, Robert Klein Time, which ran on the USA Network until 1988.
Klein hosted Monty Python Live at Aspen, a reunion and tribute show for the five surviving members of the British comedy troupe, in a special that appeared on HBO in 1998.

Robert Loggia

Born Salvatore Loggia on January 3, 1930) is an American actor and director. He was nominated for an Academy Award for Best Supporting Actor for *Jagged Edge*.
Loggia, an Italian American, was born on Staten Island on January 3, 1930, the son of Beniamino Loggia, a shoemaker, and Elena Blandino, a homemaker, both of whom were born in Sicily, Italy. After studying atWagner College and journalism at the University of Missouri (class of 1951) and serving in the U.S. Army, he began a long career as a supporting player.Bob and Doug McKenzie (sketch actors).

Bob and Doug McKenzie

They are a pair of fictional Canadian brothers who hosted "Great White North", a sketch which was introduced on SCTV for the show's third season when it moved to CBC **in 1980.** Bob is played by Rick Moranis and Doug is played by Dave Thomas. Although created originally as filler to both satisfy and mock network Canadian content demands, the duo became a pop culture phenomenon in both Canada and the United States.The characters were later revived for an animated series, Bob & Doug, which premiered on Global in 2009.

Chapter 4- Television and Film

Robert Mitchum (actor)

Robert Charles Durman Mitchum (August 6, 1917 – July 1, 1997) was an American film actor, author, composer and singer. Mitchum rose to prominence for his starring roles in several classic films noir, and is generally considered a forerunner of the anti-heroes prevalent in film during the 1950s and 1960s. His best-known films include The Story of G.I. Joe (1945), Crossfire (1947), Out of the Past (1947), The Night of the Hunter (1955), Cape Fear (1962), and El Dorado (1966).

Mitchum was born in Bridgeport, Connecticut into a Methodist family. His mother, Ann Harriet Mitchum (née Gunderson), was a Norwegian immigrant and sea captain's daughter, and his father, James Thomas Mitchum, was of Scots-Ulster descent and was a shipyard and railroad worker.

Mitchum is rated #23 on the American Film Institute's list of the 50 greatest American screen legends of all time (25 greatest males/25 greatest females).

Bob Newhart (actor, comedian)

George Robert "Bob" Newhart (born September 5, 1929) is an American stand-up comedian and actor. Noted for his deadpan and slightly stammering delivery, Newhart came to prominence in the 1960s when his album of comedic monologues The Button-Down Mind of Bob Newhart was a worldwide bestseller and reached number one on the Billboard pop album chart—it remains the 20th best-selling comedy album in history. The follow-up album, The Button-Down Mind Strikes Back! was also a massive success, and the two albums held the Billboard number one and number two spots simultaneously.

Newhart later went into acting, starring in two long-running and award-winning situation comedies, first as psychologist Dr. Robert "Bob" Hartley on the 1970s sitcom The Bob Newhart Show and then as innkeeper Dick Loudon on the 1980s sitcom Newhart. He also had two short-lived sitcoms in the nineties titled Bob and George and Leo. Newhart also appeared in film roles such as Major Major in Catch-22 and Papa Elf in Elf. He provided the voice of Bernard in the Walt Disney animated films The Rescuers (1977) and The Rescuers Down Under (1990). In 2004 he played the library head Judson in The Librarian, a character which continued in 2014 to the TV seriesThe Librarians. In 2011, Newhart made a cameo in the film Horrible Bosses, and in 2013 he guest starred in three episodes of The Big Bang Theory, for one of which he won his first Primetime Emmy Award on September 15, 2013.

Chapter 4- Television and Film

On February 20, 2015, Newhart was honored with the Publicists of the International Cinematographers Guild Lifetime Achievement Award.

Bob Odenkirk (actor)

Robert John "Bob" Odenkirk (born October 22, 1962) is an American actor, comedian, writer, director, and producer. He co-created and co-starred in the HBO sketch comedy series Mr. Show with Bob and David and is also known for his role as lawyer Saul Goodman on the AMC crime drama series Breaking Bad and its spin-off seriesBetter Call Saul.

In the 1980s and 1990s, Odenkirk worked as a writer for such television shows as Saturday Night Live, Late Night with Conan O'Brien, Get a Life, The Ben Stiller Showand The Dennis Miller Show. In the mid-1990s, Odenkirk and David Cross created the Emmy-nominated sketch comedy program Mr. Show with Bob and David, which ran for four seasons and ultimately became a cult success. In the early 2000s, Odenkirk discovered the comedy duo Tim & Eric and produced their television seriesTom Goes to the Mayor and Tim and Eric Awesome Show, Great Job! He has directed three films: Melvin Goes to Dinner (2003), Let's Go to Prison (2006) and The Brothers Solomon (2007).

Bobby Van (actor)
Bobby Van (December 6, 1928 – July 31, 1980) was a musical actor, best known for his career on Broadway in the 1950s and 1970s. He was also a game show hoBobby Van was born Robert Jack Stein to vaudeville parents in The Bronx, New York City, and grew up backstage, witnessing many memorable Depression-era acts. Originally, Van took King as his stage name (after his father's stage name, from the trio "Gordon, Reed and King"). He finally opted for Van, supposedly after seeing aVan Johnson poster hanging in his sister's bedroom.

Robert Wagner (actor)

Robert John Wagner, Jr. born February 10, 1930) is an American actor of stage, screen, and television, best known for starring in the television shows It Takes a Thief (1968–70), Switch (1975–78), and Hart to Hart (1979–84). He also had a recurring role as Teddy Leopold on the TV sitcom Two and a Half Men and has a recurring role as Anthony DiNozzo Sr. on the police procedural NCIS.

In movies, Wagner is known for his role as Number Two in the Austin Powers trilogy of films (1997, 1999, 2002), as well as for A Kiss Before Dying, The Pink Panther,Harper, The Towering Inferno and many more. Wagner's autobiography, Pieces of My Heart: A Life, written with author Scott Eyman, was published on September 23, 2008.

Robert Redford (actor, director)

Charles Robert Redford Jr. (born August 18, 1936), better known as Robert Redford, is an American actor, film director, producer, businessman, environmentalist, philanthropist, and a founder of the Sundance Film Festival. He has received two Academy Awards: one in 1981 for directing Ordinary People, and one for Lifetime Achievement in 2002. In 2010, he was awarded French Knighthood in the Legion d'Honneur.

Redford's career began in New York. He started his acting career in 1959 as a guest star on numerous TV programs, including The Untouchables, Perry Mason, Alfred Hitchcock Presents, and The Twilight Zone, among others. He earned an Emmy nomination as Best Supporting Actor for his performance in The Voice of Charlie Pont (ABC, 1962). Redford's biggest Broadway success was as the stuffy newlywed husband of Elizabeth Ashley in Neil Simon's Barefoot in the Park (1963). Redford made his film debut in War Hunt (1962). Inside Daisy Clover (1965) won him a Golden Globe for best new star. He starred in George Roy Hill's Butch Cassidy and the Sundance Kid (1969), which was a huge success and made him a major star. In 1972, he had a critical and box office hit with Jeremiah Johnson (1972) and the biggest hit of his career; the blockbuster crime caper The Sting (1973), for which he was also nominated for an Oscar. The popular and acclaimed All the President's Men (1976), was a landmark film for Redford.

Bob Steele (actor)

Bob Steele (January 23, 1907 – December 21, 1988) was an American actor. He was born Robert Adrian Bradbury in Portland, Oregon, into a vaudeville family. His parents were Robert North Bradbury (1886–1949) and the former Nieta Catherine Quinn (1886–1978). After years of touring, the family settled in Hollywood, California, in the late 1910s, where his father soon found work in the movies, first as an actor, later as a director. By 1920, Robert Bradbury hired Bob and his twin brother, Bill (1907–1971), as juvenile leads for a series of adventure movies titled The Adventures of Bob and Bill.

Chapter 4- Television and Film

Robert Lane "Bob" Saget

Saget (born May 17, 1956) is an American stand-up comedian, actor and television host. Although he is best known for his family-friendly roles asDanny Tanner on Full House (1987–95) and the original host of America's Funniest Home Videos (1989–97), Saget is also known for his adult-oriented stand-up routine. He also provided the voice of the future Ted Mosby on How I Met Your Mother from 2005 to 2014

Saget was born in Philadelphia to a Jewish family. His father, Benjamin (August 28, 1917 – January 30, 2007), was a supermarket executive, and his mother, Rosalyn "Dolly" (February 12, 1925 – February 15, 2014), was a hospital administrator. Saget lived in California before moving back to Philadelphia and graduating from high school.] Saget originally intended to become a doctor, but his Honors English teacher, Elaine Zimmerman, saw his creative potential and urged him to seek a career in film.

Saget attended Temple University's film school, where he created *Through Adam's Eyes*, a black-and-white film about a boy who received reconstructive facial surgery, and was honored with an award of merit in the Student Academy Awards. He graduated with a B.A. in 1978. Saget intended to take graduate courses at the University of Southern California but quit a few days later. Saget describes himself at the time in an article by Glenn Esterly in the 1990 *Saturday Evening Post*: "I was a cocky, overweight twenty-two-year-old. Then I had a gangrenous appendix taken out, almost died, and I got over being cocky or overweight." Saget talked about his burst appendix on *Anytime with Bob Kushell*, saying that it happened on the Fourth of July, at the UCLA Medical Center and that they at first just iced the area for seven hours before taking it out and finding that it had become gangrenous.

Buffalo Bob Smith

Buffalo Bob Smith (born Robert Emil Schmidt; November 27, 1917 – July 30, 1998) was the host of the children's show Howdy Doody.Born in Buffalo, New York, he attended Masten Park High School. Buffalo Bob got his start in radio in Buffalo. He started at WGR (AM) but switched from WGR toWBEN's late morning radio slot in 1943, as part of a move which also brought Clint Buehlman's early morning show over from WGR to WBEN at the same time. (The WBEN morning slot had opened when its host, future NBC-TV personality Jack Parr was drafted into the military.) WBEN was seeking to break WGR's #1 position in local popularity and shaking the position of network-fed Don McNeil's Breakfast Club's grip on ratings for the 9 am time slot was an important part of the plan. WBEN first brought Clint Buehlman's popular early morning show, which ended at 9am, followed by 15 minutes of local news, over from WGR.

Then, Buffalo Bob appeared at 9:15 am. Within a period of time, Smith had won the #1 spot in late mornings for WBEN and McNeil tumbled to second in the Buffalo market. Both Buehlman's and Smith's shows were produced by Ed Huber. Smith's popularity in Buffalo won the attention of NBC, which brought him to New York after the war to host early mornings on flagship station WNBC, a post he held through the early 1950s before concentrating on television. For a time between 1947 and 1953 he appeared mornings on WNBC even while hosting and producing the daily Howdy Doody children's show on the NBC television network in late afternoons.

SpongeBob/ SquarePants

SpongeBob SquarePants is an American animated television series created by marine biologist and animator Stephen Hillenburg. The series chronicles the adventures and endeavors of the title character and his various friends in the fictional underwater city of Bikini Bottom. The series' popularity has made it a media franchise, as well as the highest rated series to ever air on Nickelodeon, and the most distributed property of MTV Networks. The media franchise has generated $8 billion in merchandising revenue for Nickelodeon.

Many of the ideas for the series originated in an unpublished, educational comic book titled The Intertidal Zone, which Hillenburg created in the mid-1980s. He began developing SpongeBob SquarePants into a television series in 1996 upon the cancellation of Rocko's Modern Life, and turned to Tom Kenny, who had worked with him on that series, to voice the titular character. SpongeBob was originally going to be named SpongeBoy, and the series was to be called SpongeBoy Ahoy! but these were both changed, as the name was already trademarked.

Bob Schieffer

Bob Lloyd Schieffer (born February 25, 1937) is an American television journalist who has been with CBS News since 1969, serving 23 years as anchor on the Saturday edition of CBS Evening News from 1973 to 1996; Chief Washington correspondent since 1982, moderator of the Sunday public affairs show Face the Nationsince 1991. From March 2005 to August 31, 2006, Schieffer was interim weekday anchor of the CBS Evening News. As of 2011, he is one of the primary substitutes forScott Pelley

Schieffer is one of the few journalists to have covered all four of the major Washington national assignments: the White House, the Pentagon, United States Department of State, and United States Congress. His career with CBS has almost exclusively dealt with national politics.

Billy Bob Thornton

Billy Bob Thornton (born August 4, 1955) is an American actor, director, writer, producer, and singer-songwriter. Thornton made his first break with co-writing and starring in the 1992 thriller One False Move and came to international attention after writing, directing, and starring in the independent drama Sling Blade (1996), for which he won an Academy Award for Best Adapted Screenplay and was nominated for an Academy Award for Best Actor. He appeared in several major film roles in the 1990s following Sling Blade, including the romantic comedy crime thriller U Turn (1997), the drama Primary Colors (1998), the science fiction disaster thrillerArmageddon (1998), and the drama A Simple Plan (1998), which earned him his third Oscar nomination.

Robert Towne

Robert Towne (born Robert Bertram Schwartz; November 23, 1934) is an American screenwriter, producer, director and actor. He was part of the New Hollywoodwave of filmmaking. His most notable work was his Academy Award-winning original screenplay for Roman Polanski's Chinatown (1974).Towne is the author of many notable film scripts, including Chinatown (1974), for which he received an Academy Award; its sequel, The Two Jakes (1990); the Oscar-nominated screenplays The Last Detail andShampoo; as well as the first two Mission Impossible films. Towne has also a "stellar reputation" in the motion-picture industry as an uncredited script doctor, having worked in this capacity on The Godfather,Bonnie and Clyde, The Parallax View, The Rock and on dozens of other Hollywood films.

Bob Weinstein

Robert "Bob" Weinstein (born October 18, 1954) is an American film producer. He is the founder and head of Dimension Films, former co-chairman of Miramax Films, and current head, with his brother Harvey Weinstein, of The Weinstein Company. Of the two Weinstein brothers, Bob has a reputation as the quieter of the two, and has focused on making commercially successful action and horror films.

Weinstein was born in Flushing, New York. He was raised in a Jewish family, the son of Max Weinstein, a diamond cutter, and Miriam (Postal). He grew up with his older brother, Harvey Weinstein, in a housing co-op named Electchester in New York City.

Bob Woodruff

Robert Warren "Bob" Woodruff (born August 18, 1961) is an American television journalist. His career in journalism dates back to 1989, and he is widely known for succeeding Peter Jennings as co-anchor of ABC News's weekday news broadcast, World News Tonight, in December 2005. In January 2006 he was critically wounded by a roadside bomb in Iraq.

Chapter 5

BOB in Sports

Chapter 5- Bob in Sports

Bob Bradley (American football)

Robert "Bob" Bradley (born March 3, 1958) is an American association football coach. He is the current manager of Stabæk in Norway's Tippeligaen. He previously managed the Egypt and the United States men's national soccer team. Before taking over the United States football national team in December 2006, he coached in the American college game and Major League Soccer, managing the Chicago Fire, MetroStars, and Chivas USA over nine seasons
His son, Michael, is a professional footballer who plays for MLS club Toronto FC and the U.S. national team.

Bob Brenly (baseball)

Robert Earl Brenly (born February 25, 1954) is an American baseball sportscaster and a former baseball player, coach and manager in Major League Baseball. He played the majority of his career as a catcher with the San Francisco Giants. After retiring as a player, he worked as a broadcaster with the Chicago Cubs, then as a coach with the Giants, then as a broadcaster for Fox. He was hired to manage the Arizona Diamondbacks for the 2001 season, and won the franchise's only championship his first year. In 2004, he was fired by the Diamondbacks and again became a broadcaster with the Cubs until 2012. He now serves as a color commentator for Diamondbacks broadcasts.

Bob Brown (offensive lineman)

Robert Stanford "Bob" Brown (born December 8, 1941, in Cleveland, Ohio), nicknamed "The Boomer" is a former American football offensive tackle in theNational Football League from 1964 through 1973. He was drafted by the Philadelphia Eagles as the second overall pick in the 1964 NFL Draft. He played for the Eagles from 1964–1968, the Los Angeles Rams from 1969–1970 NFL season, and the Oakland Raiders from 1971–1973. He played college football atNebraska. Brown was inducted into the College Football Hall of Fame in 1993. He was inducted into the Pro Football Hall of Fame in 2004.

Bob Cousy (basketball)

Robert Joseph "Bob" Cousy (born August 9, 1928) is a retired American professional basketball player. Cousy played point guard with the Boston Celtics from 1950 to 1963 and briefly with the Cincinnati Royals in the 1969–70 season. Cousy first demonstrated his basketball abilities while playing for his high school varsity team in his junior year. He obtained a scholarship to the College of the Holy Cross, where he led the Crusaders to berths in the 1948 NCAA Tournamentand 1950 NCAA Tournament and was named an NCAA All-American for 3 seasons. Cousy was initially drafted as the third overall pick in the first round of the1950 NBA Draft by the Tri-Cities Blackhawks, but after he refused to report, he was picked up by Boston. Cousy had a very successful career with the Celtics, playing on six championship teams, being voted into 13 NBA All-Star Games and 12 All-NBA First and Second Teams and winning the NBA Most Valuable Player Award in 1957.

Bob Ctvrtlik (volleyball)

Robert Jan Ctvrtlik was born July 8, 1963 in Long Beach, California) and is an American volleyball player, Olympic gold medalist, businessman and former member of the International Olympic Committee. Ctvrtlik is a 1985 graduate of Pepperdine University.

Bobby Czyz (boxer)

Robert Edward Czyz (CHEZ}; born February 10, 1962) is a retired American boxer. A New Jersey native of Polish descent, he is both a former world light heavyweight and cruiserweight champion.

Czyz was born in Orange, New Jersey. He lived in Wanaque, New Jersey and attended Lakeland Regional High School.

Nicknamed "Matinee Idol", Czyz was a member of the United States amateur boxing team whose other members died in the LOT Polish Airlines plane crash in Poland in 1980. Because of an auto accident one week before the fatal trip, Czyz was not on the plane.

Bob Dickson (golfer)

Robert B. Dickson (born January 25, 1944) is an American professional golfer who played on the PGA Tour and the Champions Tour. Dickson was born in McAlester, Oklahoma. He was introduced to golf at the age of five by his father, Ben, a club pro/manager at the McAlester Country Club, and later club pro at the Muskogee Country Club (1958–1978). He attended high school in Muskogee, and was the state 2A golf champion for three years.Dickson attended Oklahoma State University in Stillwater, Oklahoma, where he was a two-time All-American as a member of the golf team from 1964–1966. He graduated with a Bachelor of

Science degree in General Business in 1967. That year he became the first amateur golfer since 1935 to win both the U.S. Amateurand British Amateur. He turned professional and joined the PGA Tour in 1968

Robert W. Duden (golfer)

Robert W. Duden (September 5, 1920 – March 22, 1995) was an American professional golfer who played on the PGA Tour in the 1950s and 1960s. A lifelong resident of Portland, Oregon, Duden compiled a remarkable record in sectional golf competition. He won over 50 tournaments in a 40 year career that included 23 major Pacific Northwest Section events including a record 7 wins of the Pacific Northwest Senior PGA Championship. He won the Oregon Open a record eight times. In competition on the PGA Tour, Duden's best showings were three 2nd place ties between 1959 and 1964. His best finish in a major championship was T-46 at the 1954 U.S. Open. Duden invented and patented the croquet style putter, which he named "The Dude". When other well-known professionals like Sam Snead adopted this revolutionary putting technique, its popularity began to surge; however, the USGA banned it when tradionalists like Bobby Jones objected.

Bob Gibson (baseball)

Robert "Bob" Gibson (born November 9, 1935) is a retired American baseball pitcher who played 17 seasons in Major League Baseball (MLB) for the St. Louis Cardinals (1959–75). Nicknamed "Gibby" and "Hoot", Gibson tallied 251 wins, 3,117 strikeouts, and a 2.91 earned run average (ERA) during his career. A nine-time All-Star and two-time World Series champion, he won two Cy Young Awards and the 1968 National League (NL) Most Valuable Player (MVP) Award. In 1981, he was elected to the Baseball Hall of Fame in his first year of eligibility. The Cardinals retired his uniform number 45 in September 1975 and inducted him into the team Hall of Fame in 2014.

Born in Omaha, Nebraska, Gibson overcame childhood illness to excel in youth sports, particularly basketball and baseball. After briefly playing under contract to both the basketball Harlem Globetrotters team and the St. Louis Cardinals organization, Gibson decided to only continue playing baseball professionally. Once becoming a full-time starting pitcher in July 1961, Gibson began experiencing an increasing level of success, earning his first All-Star appearance in 1962. Gibson won two of three games he pitched in the 1964 World Series, then won 20 games in a season for the first time in 1965. Gibson also pitched three complete game victories in the 1967 World Series.

The pinnacle of Gibson's career was 1968, when he posted a 1.12 ERA for the season and then followed that by recording 17 strikeouts during Game 1 of the 1968 World Series. Over the course of his career, Gibson became known for his fierce competitive nature and the intimidation factor he used against opposing batters. Gibson threw a no-hitter during the 1971 season, but began experiencing swelling in his knee in subsequent seasons. After retiring as a player in 1975, Gibson later served as pitching coach for his former teammate Joe Torre. At one time a special instructor coach for the St. Louis Cardinals, Gibson was later selected for the Major League Baseball All-Century Team in 1999.

Bob Goalby (golfer)

Robert George Goalby (born March 14, 1929) is a former American professional golfer on the PGA Tour, who won the Masters Tournament in 1968, his lonemajor championship among 11 Tour wins achieved between 1958 and 1971.

Goalby was born, raised, and has lived much of his life in Belleville, Illinois. He attended the University of Illinois, where he played on the football team. He turned professional in 1952. His first Tour win came in 1958, and he won and contended steadily until 1971, when he was 42 years old.

Bob Gansler (soccer)

Bob Gansler (born July 1, 1941 in Mucsi, Hungary) is a Hungarian-born American soccer player and coach. He coached the US National Team at the 1990 World Cup, the team's first appearance at the tournament since 1950.

Gansler spent the 2007 MLS Season in Canada as an assistant coach for Toronto FC. He left the team after their successful first season to spend more time with his wife, Nancy, four sons, (Bob, Peter, Michael, and Danny) and 11 grandchildren. The grandchildren are Ben, Nicky, Erika, Alex, Andrew, Abby, Ryan, Anna, Bryan, Lennon, and Milo. Previously, Gansler coached the Kansas City Wizards, winning the club's first MLS Cup in 2000 and the US Open Cup in 2004. He also coached the Milwaukee Rampage to the A-League title in 1997. He stepped down from his coaching position with the Wizards on July 19, 2006.

Chapter 5- Bob in Sports

Bob Hartley (hockey)

Robert Hartley (born September 7, 1960) is the current head coach for the Calgary Flames in the National Hockey League. He coached the Colorado Avalanche from1998–2002, a period during which he won the Stanley Cup (2000–2001). He also coached the Atlanta Thrashers from the 2003 up until the beginning of the 2007, when he was fired after the

Thrashers got off to an 0–6 start. Hartley was enjoying a successful media career as a hockey analyst for the French-language RDS television channel, but in summer 2011 signed for the ZSC Lions, where he was the head coach in Zurich, Switzerland.Hartley and his wife, Micheline, have one daughter, Kristine and one son, Steve.Despite his anglophone-sounding name, Hartley is a Franco-Ontarian. French is his first language; his English has a marked French accent.

Bobby Holík (hockey)

Robert Holík (born January 1, 1971) is a retired Czech-American professional ice hockey center who played 18 seasons in the National Hockey League (NHL). Holík is the son of Jaroslav Holík, a Czech ice hockey world champion in 1972 and Czech national team head coach who led the under-20 team to world titles in 2000 and 2001.

Holik began his NHL career playing for the Hartford Whalers in 1990 after being selected tenth overall by them in the 1989 NHL Entry Draft. After two seasons with the Whalers, he was traded to the New Jersey Devils where he played for ten seasons, featuring as a member of the 'Crash Line' along with Mike Peluso and Randy McKay, and winning two Stanley Cups: first in 1995 and again in 2000. Prior to the 2002–03 season Holík as a free agent signed a five-year, $45 million contract with the New York Rangers.

Bob Hoover (show pilot)

Robert A. "Bob" Hoover (born January 24, 1922) is a former air show pilot and United States Air Force test pilot, known for his wide-brimmed straw hat and wide smile. In aviation circles, he is often referred to as "The pilots' pilot." Hoover learned to fly at Nashville's Berry Field while working at a local grocery store to pay for the flight training. He enlisted in the Tennessee National Guard and was sent for pilot training with the Army. During World War II, he was sent to Casablanca where his first major assignment was test flying the assembled aircraft ready for service.

He was later assigned to the Spitfire-equipped 52nd Fighter Group in Sicily. In 1944, on his 59th mission, his malfunctioning Mark V Spitfire was shot down by a Focke-Wulf Fw 190 off the coast of Southern France and he was taken prisoner. He spent 16 months at the German prison campStalag Luft 1 in Barth, Germany.

Bob Hurley (basketball)

Robert Matthew "Bob" Hurley, Sr. (born July 31, 1947) is the basketball coach at St. Anthony High School in Jersey City, New Jersey. Hurley has amassed 27 state championships and more than 1000 wins in 39 years as a coach. On February 2, 2011, Hurley became the tenth coach in high school history to win 1000 games. Five of his teams have gone undefeated, including his 2007–08 team. On April 5, 2010, he was announced as the only coach to be inducted into the Basketball Hall of Fame that year and only the third high school coach in history to be so honored; he was formally inducted on August 13 of that year. Hurley is the father of Bobby Hurley, a former All-American point guard at Duke and the Head basketball coach at University at Buffalo, and Dan Hurley, who was hired in February 2012 to coach theUniversity of Rhode Island after two years of coaching at Wagner College and nine years coaching at Newark's Saint Benedict's Preparatory School, also one of the top high school programs in the nation..

Bobby Jones (golfer)
Robert Tyre "Bobby" Jones Jr. (March 17, 1902 – December 18, 1971) was an American amateur golfer, and a lawyer by profession. Jones founded and helped design the Augusta National Golf Club, and co-founded the Masters Tournament.

Jones was the most successful amateur golfer ever to compete on a national and international level. During his peak as a golfer from 1923 to 1930, he dominated top-level amateur competition, and competed very successfully against the world's best professional golfers. Jones often beat stars such as Walter Hagen andGene Sarazen, the era's top pros. Jones earned his living mainly as a lawyer, and competed in golf only as an amateur, primarily on a part-time basis, and chose to retire from competition at age 28, though he earned significant money from golf after that, as an instructor and equipment designer.

Chapter 5- Bob in Sports

Bobby Jackson (basketball)

Bobby Jackson (born March 13, 1973) is an American retired professional basketball player. Bobby Jackson graduated from Salisbury High School in 1992. He attended Western Nebraska Community College and the University of Minnesota before being selected by the Seattle SuperSonics with the 23rd pick in the 1997 NBA draft.

As a Golden Gopher, Bobby Jackson led Minnesota to the Final Four, where they lost to the Kentucky Wildcats. He was traded to the Denver Nuggets prior to his rookie season where he played 68 games before moving on to a more familiar place in Minnesota where he donned a Timberwolves jersey for two seasons. He had his best years in Sacramento where he played for the Kings from 2000 to 2005 where he was known as "Action Jackson" and a crowd favorite. A former Sixth Man award winner, Jackson suffered an abdominal strain early in the2004–05 season that forced him to miss 51 games.

Bobby Jenks (baseball)

Jenks pitching for the Chicago White Sox in 2008.

Robert Scott "Bobby" Jenks (born March 14, 1981) is an American former professional baseball pitcher in Major League Baseball (MLB).

According to the Baseball Almanac, his fastest pitch was clocked at 102 mph on August 27, 2005, at Safeco Field. He also has a slider, changeup, and a hard, sharp-breaking curveball. Jenks is third all-time in saves by a pitcher in a White Sox uniform.

Jenks was not able to play with his teammates at Timberlake High School, in Spirit Lake, Idaho or Inglemoor High School in Kenmore, Washington, because of poor grades. Jenks did play his sophomore year of high school for Lakeland High School before Timberlake High School was opened in 1998. Since Jenks was ineligible to play the remaining years of his high school career due to poor academic performance, he played in the Prairie Cardinals American Legion program where he dominated as both a pitcher and hitter. During his final season for the Prairie Cardinals, Jenks had 123 strikeouts in 92 innings pitched.

Jenks was drafted by the Anaheim Angels in the fifth round of the 2000 Major League Baseball Draft. In one minor league game, the radar gun clocked his fastball at 100 mph. During his time with the Angels organization, Jenks spent much of his time on the disabled list because of elbow trouble. Jenks' career with the Angels ended when he was designated for assignment by the team in December 2004.

Chapter 5- Bob in Sports

Bob Johnson (baseball))

Robert Lee Johnson (November 26, 1905 – July 6, 1982), nicknamed "Indian Bob", was an American left fielder in Major League Baseball who played for threeAmerican League teams from 1933 to 1945, primarily the Philadelphia Athletics. He was the fifth player to have nine consecutive seasons of 20 or more home runs, and his 288 career HRs ranked eighth in major league history when he retired. Usually playing on inferior teams, he batted .300 five times, had eight seasons with 100 runs batted in, and finished his career among the AL's top five right-handed hitters in career RBI (1,283), runs (1,239), slugging average (.506), total bases (3501) and walks(1,075). He held the Athletics franchise record for career runs from 1942 to 1993. He also ranked among the AL leaders in games in left field (3rd, 1,592) and outfieldputouts (10th, 4,003) and assists (8th, 208) when his career ended. His elder brother Roy was a major league outfielder from 1929 to 1938.

Bob Johnson (American football)

Robert Douglas Johnson (born August 19, 1946) is a former American football center who played 12 seasons with the Cincinnati Bengals, first in theAmerican Football League, and then in the National Football League.

Johnson played college football at the University of Tennessee, where he was the first recruit of Tennessee coach Doug Dickey. He was named both All-Southeastern Conference (SEC) and All-American in 1966 and again in 1967. He earned the Jacobs Trophy, given to the SEC's best blocker, and he was named the SEC's Most Outstanding Lineman by the Birmingham Touchdown Club. Johnson finished sixth in the Heisman Trophy voting as a center.

Also in 1967, he was named an Academic All-American and was vice president of his class while earning a degree in industrial engineering.

In 1989 he was inducted into the College Football Hall of Fame.

He was the first player chosen by the Bengals in their initial season. He was the second pick overall in the draft, preceded by future Hall of Famer Ron Yary. He was the second highest-drafted center ever selected in an NFL Draft, after Ki Aldrich in 1939.

He was an AFL All-Star in 1968.

Johnson was the last original Bengal to retire, after the 1978 season. His uniform number 54 was retired by the team, and remains the only number the team has retired. However, he came out of retirement in 1979 when Bengals center Blair Bush suffered a knee injury and the Bengals asked Johnson to return as a long snapper on punts, field goals and extra points.

Following his retirement as a player, Johnson worked as a color analyst on Bengals radio from 1981 to 1985.

Bob Johnson (ice hockey, born 1931)

Robert Norman "Badger Bob" Johnson (March 4, 1931 – November 26, 1991) was an American college, international, and professional ice hockey coach. He coached the Wisconsin Badgers men's ice hockey team from 1966 to 1982, where he led the Badgers to seven appearances at the NCAA Men's Ice Hockey Championships, including three titles. During his time as the head coach at Wisconsin, Johnson also coached the United States men's national ice hockey team at the 1976 Winter Olympics and seven other major championships, including the Canada Cup and IIHF World Championships. He then coached the Calgary Flames for five seasons that included a Stanley Cup Finals loss in 1986. Johnson achieved the peak of his professional coaching career in his only season as coach of the Pittsburgh Penguins in1990–91, when the Penguins won the 1991 Stanley Cup Finals, the first Stanley Cup in team history. In August 1991, following hospitalization due to a brain aneurysm, Johnson was diagnosed with brain cancer. He died on November 26 of the same year.

Bobby Jones (golfer)

Robert Tyre "Bobby" Jones Jr. (March 17, 1902 – December 18, 1971) was an American amateur golfer, and a lawyer by profession. Jones founded and helped design the Augusta National Golf Club, and co-founded the Masters Tournament.

Jones was the most successful amateur golfer ever to compete on a national and international level. During his peak as a golfer from 1923 to 1930, he dominated top-level amateur competition, and competed very successfully against the world's best professional golfers.

Jones often beat stars such as Walter Hagen andGene Sarazen, the era's top pros. Jones earned his living mainly as a lawyer, and competed in golf only as an amateur, primarily on a part-time basis, and chose to retire from competition at age 28, though he earned significant money from golf after that, as an instructor and equipment designer.

Explaining his decision to retire, Jones said, "It [championship golf] is something like a cage. First you are expected to get into it and then you are expected to stay there. But of course, nobody can stay there." Jones is most famous for his unique "Grand Slam," consisting of his victory in all four major golf tournaments of his era (the open and amateur championships in both the U.S. & the U.K.) in a single calendar year (1930). In all Jones played in 31 majors, winning 13 and placing among the top ten finishers 27 times.

Chapter 5- Bob in Sports

After retiring from competitive golf in 1930, Jones founded and helped design the Augusta National Golf Club soon afterwards in 1933. He also co-founded the Masters Tournament, which has been annually staged by the club since 1934 (except for 1943–45, when it was canceled due to World War II). The Masters evolved into one of golf's four major championships. Jones came out of retirement in 1934 to play in the Masters on an exhibition basis through 1948. Jones played his last round of golf at Wahconah Country Club in Dalton, Massachusetts on August 15, 1948 with Bruce Crane, Rankin Furey and Bill O'Connell. Rene Clarke's portrait commemorating the event with a note from Jones stating, "This was my last effort, sorry it wasn't a better one – Bob Jones" was donated to the USGA. Citing health reasons, he quit golf permanently thereafter.

Bobby Jones was often confused with the prolific golf course designer, Robert Trent Jones, with whom he worked from time to time. "People always used to get them confused, so when they met, they decided each be called something different," Robert Trent Jones Jr. said. To help avoid confusion, the golfer was called "Bobby," and the golf course designer was called "Trent."

Bobby Jones (left-handed pitcher)

Robert Mitchell Jones (born April 11, 1972 in Orange, New Jersey) is a former Major League Baseball player who pitched in Major League Baseball from 1997-2004. He made his MLB debut on May 18, 1997, for the Colorado Rockies. Jones is currently the pitching coach for the Rockland Boulders of the independent Can-Am League.

Jones moved to Rutherford, New Jersey in 1981 and played in Rutherford Little League from 1982-1984. In 1991, he was drafted by the Milwaukee Brewers in the 44th round as a draft-and-follow. He signed prior to the 1992 draft and was assigned to Helena in the Pioneer League (Rookie), where he went 5-4.

Jones operated his own baseball academy named Bobby Jones Sports in Montville, New Jersey until it was closed down. Jones also spent time as the pitching coach for both the Don Bosco Prep and Montclair Mounties varsity baseball teams. He also worked with the Academy of Pro Players located in Hawthorne, New Jersey as a pitching instructor.

Jones made his major league debut at Shea Stadium against his boyhood team, the New York Mets. He got a no-decision in that game, won by the Mets, but earned the victory in his next start, at Coors Field against the Houston Astros.

Jones spent all of 1998 and most of 1999 with the Colorado club, splitting his time between the starting rotation and the bullpen. In early 2000, the Rockies traded Jones to the Mets, meaning he and Bobby J. Jones were now on the same roster. The two had faced each other in a 1999 game, with the Rockies' pitcher earning the victory.

Jones spent the 2001 season on the disabled list, but came back to the Mets in 2002 before being traded to the San Diego Padres, coincidentally becoming reunited there with Bobby J. Jones. He spent 2003 in Triple-A, starting with the Richmond Braves and finishing with the Omaha Royals. He was a non-roster invitee in 2004 Boston Red Sox spring training and made the big club from there, but then went into rehabilitation. After a brief stint with the independent Newark Bears of the Atlantic League in 2005, the Chicago White Sox picked him up and assigned him to Triple-A Charlotte. In 2006, Jones was signed by the Detroit Tigers, pitching for Double-A Erie.

Bobby Labonte (race car driver)

Robert Allen "Bobby" Labonte (born May 8, 1964) is an American stock car racing driver. The 2000 NASCAR Winston Cup Series champion, he competes part-time in the NASCAR Sprint Cup Series, driving the No. 32 Go FAS Racing Ford.

He and his older brother, Terry Labonte, are the only brothers to have both won Sprint Cup championships. He is also the uncle of former Nationwide Series race winner Justin Labonte. Labonte is the first driver to have won both the Winston Cup championship (2000) and the Busch Series championship (1991). He also won the IROC title in 2001.

Bob Lenarduzzi (soccer)

Robert Italo ("Bob") Lenarduzzi, OBC (born May 1, 1955 in Vancouver, British Columbia) is a former North American Soccer League star, Canadian international, and coach of the Canadian national and Olympic soccer teams. He is currently President of Vancouver Whitecaps FC. He is a member of the National Soccer Hall of Fame.

Bob Ley (sportscaster)

Bob Ley (/ˈliː/; born March 16, 1955) is a sports anchor and reporter for ESPN. A multiple Emmy Award-winner, he is the longest tenured on-air employee of the network, having joined ESPN just three days after the network's 1979 launch.

Chapter 5- Bob in Sports

Ley grew up in Bloomfield, New Jersey, where he attended Bloomfield High School. He got his start in broadcasting as a sportscaster and program director at WSOUat Seton Hall University, and interned as a production staffer at WOR-AM in New York City. After graduating magna cum laude with a Bachelor of Arts degree in Communications, Ley worked several minor broadcasting jobs, including public address announcer with the New York Cosmos soccer team, before landing his first major position with ESPN just three days after the network's launch in 1979.

In 1980, Ley hosted the first televised NCAA Selection Show, though the airing would switch to CBS two years later.

Ley currently hosts ESPN's investigative program Outside the Lines. He did host SportsCenter for much of his career at ESPN, returning on August 9, 2004 to host an "old school" edition with longtime broadcasting partner Charley Steiner. He is the primary studio host for ESPN's telecasts of major international professional soccertournaments such as the 2010 FIFA World Cup, the 2011 FIFA Women's World Cup, and the 2012 UEFA European Championship.

Bob Lee (American football)

Robert Melville Lee (born August 7, 1946 in Columbus, Ohio) is a former professional American football player. He graduated from Lowell High School (San Francisco) in 1963. Nicknamed "General" Bob Lee during a brief period of success with the Atlanta Falcons, Lee was selected in the 17th round by the Minnesota Vikings in the 1968 NFL Draft. A quarterback and punter from the University of the Pacific, Lee played in 14 NFL seasons from 1967-1981 for 3 different teams.

As a member of the Vikings, he saw action as a punter in Super Bowl IV and he threw a touchdown pass in Super Bowl XI. With starting QB Fran Tarkenton's late season injury in the 1977 season, Lee started and led the Vikings to a 14-7 win over the Los Angeles Rams in the Divisional Round of the Playoffs. The game was infamous due to the muddy conditions. Lee started the NFC Championship the next week as well against the Dallas Cowboys, but the Vikings lost 23-6. He was also a backup in Super Bowl XIV as a member of the Los Angeles Rams.

During his stint with the Falcons, he led Atlanta to a 20-14 victory over a 9-0 Viking team on Monday Night Football on November 19, 1973.

His son, Zac Lee, was the starting quarterback for the University of Nebraska for most of the 2009 season. His daughter Jenna Lee is a former anchor for Fox Business Network (which spun off from Fox News Channel), and is now an anchor on Fox News Channel.

He is one of ten quarterbacks to post both a perfect quarterback rating and a zero passer rating over the course of their careers, and is the first to have done so in the same season.

Chapter 5- Bob in Sports

Bob Mathias (American decathlete)

Robert Bruce "Bob" Mathias (November 17, 1930 – September 2, 2006) was an American decathlete, two-time Olympic gold medalist, a United States Marine Corpsofficer, actor and United States Congressman representing the state of California.

Mathias was born in Tulare, California. He attended Tulare Union High School, where he was classmates and long time friends with Sim Iness, 1952 Olympic discus gold medalist. While at Tulare Union, Mathias took up the decathlon in early 1948, at the suggestion of his track coach, Virgil Jackson. During the summer after his high school graduation, he qualified for the United States Olympic team for the 1948 Summer Olympics held in London.

In the Olympics, Mathias's naïveté about the decathlon was exposed. He was unaware of the rules in the shot put and nearly fouled out of the event. He almost failed in the high jump but was able to recover. Mathias overcame his difficulties and won the Olympic gold medal easily. At 17, he was the youngest gold medalist to win a track and field event.

Mathias continued to fare well in decathlons in the four years between the London games and the 1952 Summer Olympics in Helsinki. In 1948, Mathias won the James E. Sullivan Award as the nation's top amateur athlete, but because his scholastic record in high school did not match his athletic achievement, he spent a year at The Kiski School, a well-respected all-boys boarding school in Saltsburg, Pennsylvania. He then entered Stanford University in 1949, played college football for two years and was a member of Phi Gamma Delta fraternity. Mathias set his first decathlon world record in 1950 and led Stanford to a Rose Bowl appearance in 1952. After graduating from Stanford in 1953 with a BA in Education, Mathias spent two and a half years in the U.S. Marine Corps. He was promoted to the rank of captain and was honorably discharged.

At Helsinki, Mathias asserted himself as one of the world's best athletes. He won the decathlon by 912 points, an astounding margin, becoming the first to successfully defend an Olympic decathlon title. He returned to the United States as a national hero. In 1952, he was, therefore, the first person to ever compete in an Olympics and a Rose Bowl the same year. After the 1952 Olympics, Mathias retired from athletic competition. He later became the first director of the United States Olympic Training Center, a post he held from 1977 to 1983.

He and his wife Melba can be seen on the 29th April 1954 edition of You Bet Your Life. During the discussion he mentions a forthcoming film in which the couple played themselves, called The Bob Mathias Story. He also starred in a number of mostly cameo-type roles in a variety of movies and TV shows throughout the 1950s. In the 1959-1960 television season, Mathias played Frank Dugan, with costars Keenan Wynn as Kodiak and Chet Allen as Slats, in the NBC adventure series The Troubleshooters, which focused twenty-six episodes on events at construction sites. In 1960, he also appeared playing an athletic Theseus in an Italian "peplum," or sword-and-sandal, film: Minotaur, the Wild Beast of Crete.

Bob McLeod (American football)

Robert Don "Bob" McLeod (born November 10, 1938 in Sweetwater, Texas) is a former professional American football player. A 6'5", 232 lbs. tight end fromAbilene Christian University, McLeod was drafted by the American Football League's Houston Oilers in 1961. McLeod played 9 seasons in professional football, from 1961-1966.

Bobby Moore

Robert Frederick Chelsea "Bobby" Moore OBE (12 April 1941 – 24 February 1993) was an English professional footballer. He captained West Ham Unitedfor more than ten years and was captain of the England team that won the 1966 World Cup. He is widely regarded as one of the greatest defenders of all time, and was cited by Pelé as the greatest defender that he had ever played against. Moore is a member of the World Team of the 20th Century.

He won a total of 108 caps for the England team, which at the time of his international retirement in 1973 was a national record. This record was later broken by 125-cap goalkeeper Peter Shilton. Moore's total of 108 caps continued as a record for outfield players until 28 March 2009, when David Beckham gained his 109th cap.

Bob Murphy (golfer)

Robert Joseph Murphy, Jr. (born February 14, 1943) is an American professional golfer who was formerly a member of the PGA Tour and currently plays on theChampions Tour. Murphy has won 21 tournaments as a professional.

Murphy was born in Brooklyn, New York. He was a standout pitcher in his youth, and as a teen led his high school baseball team to the state championship in 1960. After suffering a football injury (which also ended his baseball career), Murphy got started in golf.

Chapter 5- Bob in Sports

Bob Murphy (baseball)

Robert J. Murphy (December 26, 1866 – December 13, 1904) was a pitcher in Major League Baseball in 1890 for the New York Giants and Brooklyn Gladiators.

Bob Murphy (ice hockey)

Bob Murphy (born January 27, 1951) is a Canadian retired professional ice hockey player. He was selected by the Vancouver Canucks in the 11th round (102nd overall) of the 1971 NHL Amateur Draft.

Born in 1951 in Toronto, Ontario, Murphy began his professional career in 1971 with the Syracuse Blazers of the Eastern Hockey League, and played five seasons in the minor leagues before retiring following the 1975-76 season as a member of the Maine Nordiques of the North American Hockey League.

Murphy was known as a gritty offensive forward who played 298 professional games, scoring 113 goals and 268 points, while racking up 247 penalty minutes.

Bob Neal (Cleveland sportscaster)

Bob Neal was an American sportscaster who worked primarily in Cleveland, Ohio. He broadcast the Cleveland Indians on radio 1957–1961 and 1965–1972, and on television 1952–1953 and 1962–1964. He was also the original broadcaster for Cleveland Browns football games on radio and television starting in 1946 and continuing through 1951. He handled the 1954 Orange Bowl game for CBS television, 1955 and 1956 World Series for Mutual radio and the 1957 World Series for NBC radio.

Bob Neal also worked as a sportscaster for KYW-TV (now WKYC-TV) in Cleveland, appearing alongside weatherman Joe Finan; occasionally, fellow sportscaster Jim Graner would fill in for Neal.

Bob Neal (Atlanta sportscaster)

Bob Neal has done it all. Forty years in television and radio at the national and local level. Currently, Bob is engaged in teaching sports journalism through a variety of outlets and is the anchor of the syndicated "Play To Win" NFL and college football show, produced independently and aired on a variety of stations, including Fox 5 in Atlanta. Neal has also been a familiar voice for Turner Sports on its national NBA coverage forTNT and TBS for telecasts for 23 years.

Neal's lengthy resume includes play-by-play work for NBA and college football games on NBC. Along with work for TNT and TBS for PGA Tour events, NCAA football, Atlanta Braves, Atlanta Hawks and World Cupsoccer. Previously, Neal was the radio voice of the NFL Atlanta Falcons (1975–81, 1995–97) and news and sports director of WXIA-TV in Atlanta.

Bob has been the anchor of Talkin' Football, Talkin' Hoops, SEC Hoops Tonight and offered play-by-play for college football, basketball and baseball for the Comcast Sports Network, a division of the NBC Sports Group, seen in 13 states.

In addition to his current hosting of Play To Win, his studio hosting experience include Football Saturday on TBS, the 1986 and 1990 Goodwill Games and TNT's Sunday night NFL broadcasts. Neal's long tenured association with Turner Sports began in 1977, producing and hosting "'Sports Week, on TBS, the first national sports show on cable.

Neal's accolades include five Georgia Area Emmys, three Associated Press Awards, and a share of five national Emmys for his role in Goodwill Games telecasts. Neal is also the recipient of two Cable ACE Awards for SEC Football and NBA Coverage as well as the Masters Water Ski Tournament for Turner Sports. Neal is the 2012 recipient of the Lindsey Nelson Award, in recognition of career contributions to broadcasting, presented by the National Football Foundation. Most recently Neal was honored as Distinguished Journalism Alumni by Northern Illinois University.

Bobby Nichols

Robert Herman Nichols (born April 14, 1936) is an American professional golfer, best known for winning the PGA Championship in 1964.

Born and raised in Louisville, Kentucky, Nichols attended St. Xavier High School. While in high school, Nichols and several other youths were involved in an automobile accident resulting from a 100 mph (160 km/h) joy ride. He suffered serious injuries including a broken pelvis, concussion, back and internal injuries, and was hospitalized 96 days. His legs were also paralyzed for about two weeks, but he was able to regain full use of his legs after intensive physical therapy. Nichols later played on the Aggies golf team at Texas A&M University in the Southwest Conference.

Nichols began playing on the PGA Tour in 1960 and recorded 12 victories, one of which, the PGA National Team Championship, was not fully recognized until 2012. He was a member of the Ryder Cup team in1967, and his best year on tour was 1974 when he won twice, earned $124,747 and finished 14th on the money list. Nichols, Jerry Heard, and Lee Trevino were struck by lightning at the Western Open on Friday, June 27, 1975. All three men came back to play professional golf. Nichols has had 12 holes-in-one in his professional career.

The 1964 PGA Championship was played at the Columbus Country Club in Columbus, Ohio. Nichols won with a 271 total, three shots ahead of runners-up Arnold Palmer and defending champion Jack Nicklaus, playing in his hometown. This was a record low score for the PGA Championship and it stood for 30 years, until broken by Nick Price's 269 in 1994. Nichols was the first wire-to-wire winner since the PGA Championship switched format from match play to stroke play in 1958. He came close to winning a second major at the Masters in 1967, finishing second to his lifelong friend, Gay Brewer.

After turning 50 in 1986, Nichols played on the Senior PGA Tour, now the Champions Tour. He had numerous top-10 finishes but only one victory – the Southwestern Bell Classic in 1989, when he defeated Orville Moody on the third hole of a playoff.

Bobby Nichols Golf Course is a 9-hole municipal course that is part of Waverly Park in Louisville, southwest of downtown. (38.126°N 85.838°W) The back tees are set at 6,970 yards (6,370 m) with a rating of 72.0 and a slope of 130.

Bob Nystrom (hockey)

Robert Thore Nystrom (born October 10, 1952) is a retired professional ice hockey right winger. He played for the New York Islanders of the National Hockey League(NHL) from 1972–86. He is best remembered as having scored the winning goal at the 7:11 mark of overtime to give the New York Islanders the 1980 Stanley Cup title. This signaled the first of four straight championships for the club. He was also among the last NHL players to not wear a helmet during a game.

Playing his minor hockey in Hinton, Alberta, Nystrom is immortalized on the town's wall of fame. He is arguably the most successful NHL player from the geographical area that yielded the likes of Dave Scatchard and Dean McAmmond.

His son Eric plays professional hockey for the Nashville Predators of the NHL, and previously played for the Calgary Flames, Minnesota Wild, and Dallas Stars.

Chapter 5- Bob in Sports

Bobby Richardson (baseball)

Robert Clinton "Bobby" Richardson (born August 19, 1935) is a former second baseman in Major League Baseball who played for the New York Yankees from 1955through 1966. Batting and throwing right-handed, he was a superb defensive infielder, as well as something of a clutch hitter, who played no small role in the Yankee baseball dynasty of his day. He is the only World Series MVP ever to be selected from the losing team. He wore the uniform number 1 for the majority of his career (1958–1966).

Richardson debuted on August 5, 1955. He racked up 1,432 hits in his career, with a lifetime batting average of .266, 34 home runs and 390 RBIs. He won a Gold Glove at second base each year from 1961-65 (not until Robinson Canó in 2010 would another Yankee second baseman win a Gold Glove) while forming a top double playcombination with shortstop and roommate Tony Kubek. With the light-hitting but superb-fielding Yankee third baseman Clete Boyer, Richardson and Kubek gave the Yankees arguably the best defensive infield in baseball. His most famous defensive play came at the end of the 1962 World Series, mentioned below, when Richardson made a clutch catch of a Willie McCovey line drive that prevented Willie Mays and Matty Alou from scoring the runs that would have beaten the Yankees and given the Series to the San Francisco Giants.

Richardson's 12-year career statistics also include 643 runs scored and 73 stolen bases. He also had 196 doubles and 37 triples.

Bob Rush (American football)

Robert Jeffrey Rush (born February 27, 1955 in Santa Monica, California) is a former professional American football center. He played in the National Football League for the San Diego Chargers (1977–1982) and the Kansas City Chiefs (1983–1985). He played college football for the University of Memphis.

Bob Rush (baseball)

Robert Ransom Rush (December 21, 1925 – March 19, 2011) was a professional baseball player who pitched in Major League Baseball from 1948 to 1960. Rush played for the Milwaukee Braves, Chicago Cubs, and the Chicago White Sox.

On June 11, 1950, Rush and pitcher Warren Spahn of the Braves each stole a base against each other; no opposing pitchers again stole a base in the same game until May 3, 2004, when Jason Marquis and Greg Maddux repeated the feat.

Rush was an All-Star selection in 1950 and 1952. Rush was born in Battle Creek, Michigan, and died in Mesa, Arizona.

Bob Sapp

Robert Malcolm "Bob" Sapp (born September 22, 1973) is an American professional wrestler, actor, comedian and former American football player best known for his career as a kickboxer and mixed martial artist. Sapp has a combined fight record of 22–35–1, mostly fighting in Japan. He is well known in Japan, where he has appeared in numerous commercials, television programs, and various other media, and has released a music CD, It's Sapp Time. He also appeared in an episode of theHBO program Real Sports with Bryant Gumbel. He is currently working sporadically for various MMA promotions in the U.S., Japan, and Europe.He would be the first black man to hold the IWGP heavyweight championship.

Bob Shearer

Robert A. Shearer (born 25 May 1948) is an Australian professional golfer and golf course architect.Shearer was born in Melbourne, Victoria. He won the 1969 Australian Amateur and turned pro in 1970.

Shearer won the PGA Tour of Australia Order of Merit four times: 1974, 1977, 1981, 1982. He spent five years on the European Tour and then nine on the PGA Tour. His career year was 1982 when he won the Australian Open and his sole PGA Tour event, the Tallahassee Open. He had 18 top-10 finishes in PGA Tour events. His best finish in a major championship was a T-7 at the 1978 Open Championship.

Today he splits his time between his golf course design work and the European Seniors Tour.

Bobby Thompson (baseball)

Bobby La Rue Thompson ["Bull"] (November 3, 1953 – April 25, 2011) was an outfielder in Major League Baseball, playing mainly at centerfield for the Texas Rangers during the 1978 season. Listed at 5' 11", 175 lb., Thompson was a switch-hitter and threw right-handed. He was born in Charlotte, North Carolina.

Following his graduation from Harding University High School, Thompson became the first African American born in Charlotte to join the Major Leagues. He was selected by the Texas Rangers in the 1972 amateur draft, and played six years in the Rangers Minor league system before joining the big team on April 16, 1978.

In his only major league season, Thompson served as a reserve outfielder for Al Oliver, Juan Beníquez and Bobby Bonds, being also used in pinch-hitting and pinch-running duties while appearing in 64 games. He hit a .225 average (27-for-120), including three doubles, three triples, two home runs and seven stolen bases, while driving in 12 runs and scoring 23 times. He played his last game on September 25. In a six-season minor league career, he hit .273 and 29 home runs in 520 games. Thompson died at his residence in Charlotte at the age of 57.

Bob Uecker

Robert George "Bob" Uecker (/ˈjuːkər/ EWK-ər; born January 26, 1934) is a retired American Major League Baseball player, later a sportscaster, comedian and actor. Uecker was given the title of "Mr. Baseball" by TV talk show host Johnny Carson. Since 1971 Uecker has served as a play-by-play announcer for Milwaukee Brewersradio broadcasts.

Though he has sometimes joked that he was born on an oleo run to Illinois, Uecker was born and raised in Milwaukee, Wisconsin. He grew up watching the minor-league Milwaukee Brewers at Borchert Field. He signed a professional contract with his hometown Milwaukee Braves in 1956 and made his Major League Baseball debut as a catcher with the club in 1962. A below-average hitter, he finished with a career batting average of .200. He was generally considered to be a sound defensive player and committed very few errors in his Major League career as a catcher, completing his career with a fielding percentage of .981. However, in 1967, despite playing only 59 games, he led the league in passed balls and is still on the top 10 list for most passed balls in a season. At least a partial explanation is that he spent a good deal of the season catching knuckleballer Phil Niekro. He often joked that the best way to catch a knuckleball was to wait until it stopped rolling and pick it up. Uecker also played for the St. Louis Cardinals (and was a member of the 1964 World Champion club) and Philadelphia Phillies before returning to the Braves, who had by then moved to Atlanta. His six-year Major League career concluded in 1967.

Perhaps the biggest highlight of Uecker's career was when he hit a home run off future Hall of Famer Sandy Koufax after which Uecker joked that he always thought that home run would keep Koufax from getting into the Hall of Fame.

Chapter 5- Bob in Sports

Bobby Valentine

Robert John "Bobby" Valentine (born May 13, 1950) nicknamed "Bobby V" is a former American professional baseball player and manager. He is currently the athletic director at Sacred Heart University. Valentine played for the Los Angeles Dodgers (1969, 1971–72), California Angels (1973–75), New York Mets (1977–78), and Seattle Mariners (1979) in MLB. He managed the Texas Rangers (1985–92) and the New York Mets (1996–2002) of MLB, as well as the Chiba Lotte Marines of Nippon Professional Baseball (1995, 2004–09), and Boston Red Sox (2012).

Valentine has also served as the Director of Public Safety & Health for the city of Stamford, Connecticut and an analyst for ESPN Sunday Night Baseball. In February 2013, CBSSports.com hired Bobby Valentine to represent its Fantasy Sports business including running a viral marketing campaign in which he made fun of the many times he was fired in his career and gave fans a chance to "Hire or Fire Bobby V" one more time.

Chapter 6

BOB in Music

Chapter 6-Bob in Music

Bobby Bare (country singer/songwriter)

Robert Joseph "Bobby" Bare, Sr. (born April 7, 1935) is an American country music singer and songwriter, best known for Detroit City and 500 Miles Away from Home. He is the father of Bobby Bare, Jr., also a musician.

Bare had many failed attempts to sell his songs in the 1950s.[citation needed] He finally signed with Capitol Records and recorded a few rock and roll songs without much chart success.[citation needed] Just before he was drafted into the Army, he wrote a song called "The All American Boy" and did a demo for his friend, Bill Parsons, to learn and record. Instead of using the version Bill Parsons did later, the record company, Fraternity Records, decided to use the original demo recorded by Bobby Bare. The record reached number 2 on the Billboard Hot 100, but they made an error: the singles' labels all credited the artist as being "Bill Parsons." The same track, with the same billing error, peaked at No. 22 in the UK Singles Chart in April 1959.

Barbecue Bob (blues musician)

Robert Hicks, better known as Barbecue Bob (September 11, 1902 – October 21, 1931) was an early American Piedmont blues musician. His nickname came from the fact that he was a cook in a barbecue restaurant. One of the two extant photographs of Bob show him playing his guitar while wearing a full length white apron and cook's hat.

He was born in Walnut Grove, Georgia. He and his brother, Charlie Hicks, together with Curley Weaver, were taught how to play the guitar by Curley's mother, Savannah "Dip" Weaver. Bob began playing the 6-string guitar but picked up the 12-string guitar after moving to Atlanta, Georgia in 1923-1924. He became one of the prominent performers of the newly developing early Atlanta blues style.

In Atlanta, Hicks worked a variety of jobs, playing music on the side. While working at Tidwells' Barbecue in a north Atlanta suburb, Hicks came to the attention ofColumbia Records talent scout Dan Hornsby. Hornsby recorded him and decided to use Hicks's job as a gimmick, having him pose in chef's whites and hat for publicity photos and dubbing him "Barbecue Bob".

Chapter 6-Bob in Music

Bobby Braddock (country songwriter/producer)

Robert Valentine (Bobby) Braddock (born August 5, 1940) is an American country music songwriter and record producer. A member of the Country Music Hall of Fame and the Nashville Songwriters Hall of Fame,
Braddock has contributed numerous hit songs during more than 40 years in the industry, including 13 number-one hit singles.

Braddock was born in Lakeland, Florida to a father who was a citrus grower. Braddock spent his youth in Auburndale, Florida, where he learned to play piano and saxophone. The musician toured Florida and the South with rock and roll bands in the late 1950s and early 1960s. At the age of twenty four, Braddock moved to Nashville, Tennessee to pursue a career in Country Music.

After arriving in Nashville, Braddock joined Marty Robbins' band as a pianist in February 1965. In January of the next year, a song he wrote for Robbins, "While You're Dancing", became Braddock's first record to appear on the charts. He then signed his first of five recording contracts with major record labels and with a publishing contract with Tree Publishing Company, now Sony BMG. Braddock quickly established himself as a bankable songwriter, penning songs in the 1970s for such artists as The Statler Brothers, Tammy Wynette, George Jones, Nancy Sinatra, Johnny Duncan, Willie Nelson, Tanya Tucker, Jerry Lee Lewis, and Tommy Overstreet.

Braddock continued his successful songwriting career well into the 21st century, writing songs recorded by artists including Lacy J. Dalton, T.G. Sheppard, John Anderson, Mark Chesnutt, and Tracy Lawrence. Braddock sometimes co-wrote songs with Curly Putman or Sonny Throckmorton, fellow members of the Nashville Songwriters Hall of Fame.
As a producer, Braddock's greatest success thus far is the discovery of country singer Blake Shelton, securing a recording deal in 2001. Braddock is credited as producer for several of Shelton's number-one country hits, including his debut single "Austin" which spent five weeks at the top of the charts.

Also in 2001 Braddock penned the song "I Wanna Talk About Me", intended for Shelton but eventually recorded by Toby Keith. "I Wanna Talk About Me" topped the Billboard Country Charts for five weeks in 2002.

In March 2007, Braddock released a memoir recounting his early life in pre-Disney World Central Florida, titled *Down in Orbundale: A Songwriters Youth in Old Florida,*[1] published by Louisiana State University Press. Braddock currently resides in Nashville and continues to write songs for publishing company, Sony/ATV.

Chapter 6-Bob in Music

Bob Dylan (singer/songwriter)

Bob Dylan was born Robert Allen Zimmerman, May 24, 1941 and is an American singer-songwriter, artist, and writer. He has been influential in popular music and culture for more than five decades. Much of his most celebrated work dates from the 1960s when his songs chronicled social unrest, although Dylan repudiated suggestions from journalists that he was a spokesman for his generation. Nevertheless, early songs such as "Blowin' in the Wind" and

"The Times They Are a-Changin'" became anthems for the American civil rights and anti-war movements. Leaving his initial base in the American folk music revival, Dylan's six-minute single "Like a Rolling Stone" altered the range of popular music in 1965. His mid-1960s recordings, backed by rock musicians, reached the top end of the United States music charts while also attracting denunciation and criticism from others in the folk movement.

Dylan's lyrics have incorporated various political, social, philosophical, and literary influences. They defied existing pop music conventions and appealed to the burgeoning counterculture. Initially inspired by the performances of Little Richard, and the songwriting of Woody Guthrie, Robert Johnson and Hank Williams, Dylan has amplified and personalized musical genres. His recording career, spanning 50 years, has explored the traditions in American song—from folk, blues, and country togospel, rock and roll, and rockabilly to English, Scottish, and Irish folk music, embracing even jazz and the Great American Songbook. Dylan performs with guitar, keyboards and harmonica. Backed by a changing line-up of musicians, he has toured steadily since the late 1980s on what has been dubbed the Never Ending Tour. His accomplishments as a recording artist and performer have been central to his career, but his greatest contribution is considered his songwriting.

Since 1994, Dylan has published six books of drawings and paintings, and his work has been exhibited in major art galleries. As a musician, Dylan has sold more than 100 million records, making him one of the best-selling artists of all time; he has received numerous awards including Grammy, Golden Globe and Academy Award; he has been inducted into the Rock and Roll Hall of Fame, Minnesota Music Hall of Fame, Nashville Songwriters Hall of Fame, and Songwriters Hall of Fame. The Pulitzer Prize jury in 2008 awarded him a special citation for "his profound impact on popular music and American culture, marked by lyrical compositions of extraordinary poetic power." In May 2012, Dylan received the Presidential Medal of Freedom from Barack Obama.

Chapter 6-Bob in Music

Bobby Darin (singer)

(born Walden Robert Cassotto; May 14, 1936 – December 20, 1973) was an American singer, songwriter, and actor of film and television. He performed in a range of music genres, including pop, rock'n'roll, folk, and country.

He started as a songwriter for Connie Francis, and recorded his own first million-seller "Splish Splash" in 1958. This was followed by "Dream Lover", "Mack the Knife", and "Beyond the Sea", which brought him world fame. In 1962, he won a Golden Globe for his first film Come September, co-starring his first wife, Sandra Dee.

Throughout the 1960s, he became more politically active and worked on Robert Kennedy's Democratic presidential campaign. He was present on the night of June 4/5, 1968, at the Ambassador Hotel in Los Angeles at the time of Kennedy's assassination. The same year, he discovered that he had been brought up by his grandmother, not his mother, and that the girl he had thought to be his sister was actually his mother. These events deeply affected Darin and sent him into a long period of seclusion.

Although he made a successful television comeback, his health was beginning to fail, as he had always expected, following bouts of rheumatic fever in childhood. This knowledge of his vulnerability had always spurred him on to exploit his musical talent while still young. He died at age 37, following a heart operation in Los Angeles.

Bob Ezrin (music producer)

Robert Alan "Bob" Ezrin (born March 25, 1949) is a Canadian music producer and keyboardist, best known for his work with Lou Reed, Alice Cooper, Kiss, Pink Floyd,Peter Gabriel, and Phish. As of 2010, Ezrin's career in music had spanned four decades and his production work continued into the 21st century, with acts such asDeftones and Thirty Seconds to Mars. After co-founding interactive media company, 7th Level, in 1993, Ezrin has branched out into philanthropy and activism, with music also introduced into this realm of his life, underpinning projects such as Music Rising and Young Artists for Haiti. Ezrin is also involved in education, co-founding the Nimbus School of Recording Arts in 2009.

Ezrin is the winner of a Juno Award and was inducted into the Canadian Music Hall of Fame in April 2004.

Chapter 6-Bob in Music

Bob Ferguson (musician)

Robert Bruce "Bob" Ferguson, Sr. (December 30, 1927 – July 22, 2001) was an American country music songwriter and record producer who was instrumental in establishing Nashville, Tennessee as a center of country music. He was also a movie producer, and Choctaw Indian historian. Ferguson is best known for writing the bestselling songs "On the Wings of a Dove" and "The Carroll County Accident". The "Carroll County Accident" won the Country Music Association Song of the Year in 1969. In 1983 "Wings of a Dove" was featured in the movie Tender Mercies starring Robert Duvall. In 1987, Broadcast Music Incorporated (BMI) awarded Ferguson with the "million air" plays for the "Wings of a Dove."

The country song "Carroll County Accident", recorded by Porter Wagoner, made No. 2 on the Billboard country singles chart (No. 92 pop) and No. 1 on the Cash Boxcountry singles chart. The tune was also recorded by Wagoner's longtime duet partner Dolly Parton. Ferguson married twice, first to Harvie June Van (1950s/60s) then to Martha Jean Lewis (1970 to 2001).

Bob Geldof (singer/songwriter)

Robert Frederick Zenon "Bob" Geldof, was born 5 October 1951and is an Irish singer-songwriter, author, occasional actor and political activist. He rose to prominence as the lead singer of the Irish rock band The Boomtown Rats in the late 1970s and early 1980s alongside the punk rock movement. The band had hits with his compositions "Rat Trap" and "I Don't Like Mondays". He co-wrote "Do They Know It's Christmas?", one of the best-selling singles of all time, and starred inPink Floyd's 1982 film Pink Floyd – The Wall as "Pink".

Geldof is widely recognised for his activism, especially anti-poverty efforts concerning Africa. In 1984 he and Midge Ure founded the charity supergroup Band Aid to raise money for famine relief in Ethiopia. They went on to organise the charity super-concert Live Aid the following year and the Live 8 concerts in 2005. Geldof currently serves as an adviser to the ONE Campaign, founded by fellow Irishman Bono. A single father, Geldof has also been outspoken for the fathers' rights movement.

Geldof was appointed an honorary knighthood by Queen Elizabeth II, and is a recipient of the Man of Peace title which recognises individuals who have made "an outstanding contribution to international social justice and peace", among numerous other awards and nominations.

Chapter 6-Bob in Music

Bobbie Gentry

Roberta Lee Streeter (born July 27, 1944), was professionally known as Bobbie Gentry, and is an American singer-songwriter notable as one of the first female country artists to compose and produce her own material. Her songs typically drew on her Mississippi roots to compose vignettes of the Southern United States.

Gentry rose to international fame with her intriguing Southern Gothic narrative "Ode to Billie Joe" in 1967. The track spent four weeks as the No. 1 pop song on theBillboard Hot 100 chart and was fourth in the Billboard year-end chart of 1967 and earned her Grammy awards for Best New Artist and Best Female Pop Vocal Performance in 1968. Gentry charted eleven singles on the Billboard Hot 100 and four singles on the United Kingdom Top 40. Her album Fancy brought her a Grammy nomination for Best Female Pop Vocal Performance. After her first albums, she had a successful run of variety shows on the Las Vegas Strip. She lost interest in performing in the late 1970s, and since has lived privately in Los Angeles.

Robert Goulet (singer/actor)

Robert Gerard Goulet (November 26, 1933 – October 30, 2007) was an American singer and actor of French Canadian ancestry and Canadian upbringing and training after birth in Massachusetts. He originated the role of Lancelot in the 1960 Broadway musical Camelot and made numerous appearances in Las Vegas.

Goulet was born in Lawrence, Massachusetts, on Greenvile St. in the Tower Hill section, the only son of Jeanette (née Gauthier) and Joseph Georges André Goulet, a laborer. His parents were both of French Canadian ancestry. He was a descendant of French-Canadian pioneers Zacharie Cloutier and Jacques Goulet. Shortly after his father's death, 13-year-old Robert moved with his mother and sister Claire to Girouxville, Alberta, and he spent his formative years in Canada.

After living in Girouxville, Alberta, for several years, they moved to the provincial capital of Edmonton to take advantage of the performance opportunities offered in the city. There, he attended the famous voice schools founded by Herbert G. Turner and Jean Letourneau, and later became a radio announcer for radio stationCKUA. Upon graduating from Victoria Composite high school, Goulet received a scholarship to The Royal Conservatory of Music in Toronto. There, he studied voice with famed oratorio baritones, George Lambert and Ernesto Vinci. .

Chapter 6-Bob in Music

In 1952, he competed in CBC Television's Pick The Stars, ultimately making the semifinals. This led to other network appearances on shows like Singing Stars of Tomorrow, Opportunity Knocks, and the Canadian version of Howdy Doody in which he starred opposite William Shatner.

Robert Hunter (lyricist)

Robert C. Hunter (born June 23, 1941) is an American lyricist, singer-songwriter, translator, and poet, best known for his work with the Grateful Dead and for collaborating with singer-songwriter Bob Dylan.

He was born Robert Burns in San Luis Obispo, California. An early friend of Jerry Garcia, they played together in bluegrass bands (such as the Tub Thumpers) in the early sixties, with Hunter on mandolin and upright bass.

Around 1962, Hunter was an early volunteer test subject (along with Ken Kesey) for psychedelic chemicals at Stanford University's research covertly sponsored by theCIA in their MKULTRA program. [McNally 42] He was paid to take LSD, psilocybin, and mescaline and report on his experiences, which were creatively formative for him: "Sit back picture yourself swooping up a shell of purple with foam crests of crystal drops soft nigh they fall unto the sea of morning creep-very-softly mist...and then sort of cascade tinkley-bell like (must I take you by the hand, every so slowly type) and then conglomerate suddenly into a peal of silver vibrant uncomprehendingly, blood singingly, joyously resoundingbells....By my faith if this be insanity, then for the love of God permit me to remain insane." [McNally 42–43]

The first lyrics he wrote for the Grateful Dead were composed while on LSD, and mailed to the band from Arizona: a suite that would later become "China Cat Sunflower"/"The Eleven" (these were performed together for a short time). "China Cat Sunflower" would later find a partner in "I Know You Rider". After battling moderatedrug addiction, he abandoned his Joycean/Western vision quest and joined his old friend's band, the Grateful Dead, on the first weekend in September 1967, at the smallRio Nido, California, gigs. The association was at first informal, but began on an auspicious note, as that weekend he wrote the first verse of one of his better-known songs, "Dark Star". It is perhaps not a coincidence that some Deadheads argue that the Rio Nido gigs were the first in which the band accessed the full power of their psychedelic improvisation style.[citation needed]

Hunter's relationship with the band grew until he was officially a non-performing band member. When the band was inducted into the Rock and Roll Hall of Fame in 1994, Hunter was included as a band member, the only non-performer ever so honored. The majority of the Grateful Dead's original songs are Hunter/Garcia collaborations, where Garcia composed the music and Hunter wrote the lyrics. Garcia once described Hunter as "the band member who doesn't come out on stage with us." Hunter also collaborated as a lyricist with the other voices in the Dead, Bob Weir, Phil Lesh, and Ron "Pigpen" McKernan, although over time Weir, the other principal songwriter besides Garcia, switched to using John Perry Barlow as a lyricist.

Hunter called 1970's "Friend of the Devil" the closest he and Garcia came to writing a classic song. Hunter's best-known line is probably What a long, strange trip it's been, from that year's "Truckin'".

In 1974, Hunter released the solo album Tales of the Great Rum Runners featuring himself as a singer songwriter. It was followed the next year by Tiger Rose. Neither attracted a large audience. Another of his solo efforts is the extremely rare recording Jack O' Roses, containing the extended version of "Terrapin Station Suite" (sans the non-Hunter "At A Siding") and a solo rendition of "Friend of the Devil".

In 1983, Hunter convinced Relix magazine founder, Les Kippel, to start a record company. Hunter wanted an American outlet for his new project Jack O'Roses.

Bobby Jones (singer)

Bobby Jones (born September 18, 1939 in Henry, Tennessee) is a Grammy Award–winning Gospel music singer and television host from Nashville, Tennessee and the host and executive producer of several cable television's gospel music program including Bobby Jones Gospel.

Jones began his television career in 1976, when Nashville station WSM-TV (now WSMV) gave him a slot on the Sunday morning schedule with Nashville Gospel. That show continued for some 25 years, with a number of hosts.

Jones has produced programs for BET since 1980. His shows figure prominently in the channel's Sunday lineup, consistently ranking in the Top 5 of overall BET weekly programming. In addition to his work for BET, Jones produced and hosted a similar half-hour program for WDCN-TV (now WNPT), Nashville's public television outlet, during the early 1980s. The show was seen early Saturday evenings.

Bobby Jones Gospel lays claim to offering the first prime exposure to several Gospel music solo artists and groups including Kirk Franklin, Mary Mary, Yolanda Adams, and Smokie Norful. Other artists featured have included Albertina Walker, Patti Labelle, and Dorothy Norwood. Jones also hosts shows for other television networks including Bobby Jones' Next Generation on the Gospel Music Channel and Bobby Jones Presents for The Word Network.

On radio, he is the host of Bobby Jones Gospel Countdown, a two-hour weekend Gospel countdown show heard on American Urban Radio Networks, in addition to the Bobby Jones Radio Show, which is heard on Sheridan Gospel Network.

Jones also oversees the Nashville Super Choir. The choral ensemble boasts prominent soloists and serves as the vocal collective for his BET series.

Jones hosts a bi-annual International Gospel Industry Retreat in Las Vegas, Nevada and Hollywood, Florida. He also helped spearhead an initiative for the Gospel Complex for Education & Preservation in Fort Lauderdale, Florida, a museum that will host Gospel music artifacts and serve as an information center for the history of urban contemporary Gospel music.

In 1984, he won a Grammy Award for the Best Soul Gospel Performance By A Duo Or Group with Barbara Mandrell for "I'm So Glad I'm Standing Here Today." Jones is also the recipient of a Dove Award, threeStellar Awards, and a presidential commendation from President George W. Bush .

Jones has authored two books. In 2000, his memoir, Make A Joyful Noise (St. Martins Press) included chapters about his tiff with the Winans family and his personal conversations with the Rev. James Cleveland. Both topics were controversial and caused some friction with Gospel's first family and Cleveland's music organization, the Gospel Music Workshop of America. In 1999, Jones released Touched By God (Simon & Schuster), a collection of inspirational stories by top Gospel artists about how God has changed their lives. Dr. Bobby Jones, leader of The Nashville Super Choir, has now opened his own production studio, Visions, located in Nashville, TN.

Bob Marley (singer/songwriter)

Robert Nesta "Bob" Marley, OM (6 February 1945 – 11 May 1981) was a Jamaican reggae singer, songwriter, musician, and guitarist who achieved international fame and acclaim. Starting out in 1963 with the group the Wailers, he forged a distinctive songwriting and vocal style that would later resonate with audiences worldwide. The Wailers would go on to release some of the earliest reggae records with producer Lee Scratch Perry. After the Wailers disbanded in 1974, Marley pursued a solo career that culminated in the release of the album Exodus in 1977, which established his worldwide reputation and produced his status as one of the world's best-selling artists of all time, with sales of more than 75 million records. He was a committed Rastafari who infused his music with a sense of spirituality.

Chapter 6-Bob in Music

Me and Bobby McGee (song)

"Me and Bobby McGee" is a song written by Kris Kristofferson and Fred Foster, originally performed by Roger Miller. Others performed the song later, including the Grateful Dead, Kristofferson himself, and Janis Joplin who topped the U.S. singles chart with the song in 1971 after her death, making the song the second posthumous number-one single in U.S. chart history after "(Sittin' On) The Dock of the Bay" by Otis Redding. Billboard ranked Joplin's version as the No. 11 song for 1971.

In the original version of the song, Bobby is a woman. Joplin, who was allegedly a lover (but also a good friend and mentor) of Kristofferson's from the beginning of her career to her death, changed the sex and a few of the lyrics in her cover. Kristofferson stated he did not write this song for her, but the song is associated with her, especially in the line "Somewhere near Salinas, Lord, I let her slip away."

In a conversation with director Monte Hellman called "Somewhere Near Salinas" (available in the supplements to the Criterion Collection DVD release of Two-Lane Blacktop, a film in which Kristofferson's version is used on the soundtrack), Kristofferson stated that the film La Strada was an inspiration for the song and remarked on the irony of how a song inspired by a classic road movie should come to be used in another.

The title came from [producer and Monument Records founder] Fred Foster. He called one night and said, "I've got a song title for you. It's 'Me and Bobby McKee'." I thought he said "McGee". Bobby McKee was the secretary of Boudleaux Bryant, who was in the same building with Fred. Then Fred says, "The hook is that Bobby McKee is a she. How does that grab you?" (Laughs) I said, "Uh, I'll try to write it, but I've never written a song on assignment. So it took me a while to think about. " - Kris Kristofferson

The original song is essentially a road story about two drifters, the narrator and his girlfriend Bobby McGee (boyfriend in Joplin's version). He speaks about thumbing a diesel truck and singing with the driver all the way. The couple travels to California, as they grow more intimate and help each other through the hardships of life, but by the final verse, Bobby gets tired of the road life and decides to settle down.

She parts ways with the narrator who still continues his lifestyle, though he may never be happy again without her, as he would trade his life just to be with her again for just one day.

Chapter 6-Bob in Music

Robert Merrill (opera singer)

Robert Merrill (June 4, 1917 – October 23, 2004) was an American operatic baritone and actor, who was also active in the musical theatre circuit. He received the National Medal of Arts in 1993.

Merrill was born Moishe Miller, later known as Morris Miller, in the Williamsburg section of Brooklyn, New York, to tailor Abraham Miller, originally Milstein, and his wife Lillian, née Balaban, Jewish imigrants fromWarsaw, Poland.

His mother claimed to have had an operatic and concert career in Poland (a fact denied by her son in his biographies) and encouraged her son to have early voice training: he had a tendency to stutter, which disappeared when singing. Merrill was inspired to pursue professional singing lessons when he saw the baritone Richard Bonelli singing Count Di Luna in a performance of Il Trovatore at the Metropolitan Opera, and paid for them with money earned as a semi-professional pitcher.

In his early radio appearances as a crooner he was sometimes billed as Merrill Miller. While singing at bar mitzvahs and weddings and Borscht Belt resorts, he met an agent, Moe Gale, who found him work at Radio City Music Hall and with the NBC Symphony Orchestra, conducted by Arturo Toscanini. With Toscanini conducting, he eventually sang in two of the maestro's NBC broadcasts of famous operas, La traviata (with Licia Albanese, in 1946), and Un ballo in maschera (with Herva Nelli, in 1954). Both of those broadcasts were eventually released on both LP and CD by RCA Victor. His ranking as an important NBC performer is evidenced by his inclusion in NBC's 1947 promotional book, NBC Parade of Stars: As Heard Over Your Favorite NBC Station, displaying Sam Berman's caricatures of leading NBC personalities.

Merrill's 1944 operatic debut was in Verdi's Aida at Newark, New Jersey, with the famous tenor Giovanni Martinelli, then in the later stages of his long operatic career. Merrill, who had continued his vocal studies under Samuel Margolis made his debut at the Metropolitan Opera as winner of the Metropolitan Opera Auditions of the Air in 1945, as Germont in La traviata. Also in 1945, Robert Merrill recorded a 78rpm record set with Jeanette MacDonald featuring selections from the operetta Up In Central Park; MacDonald and Merrill did two duets together on this album.

In 1951, Merrill did a series of duet recordings together with the Swedish tenor Jussi Björling, including a world-renowned recording of "Au fond du temple saint" from the opera Les pêcheurs de perles by Georges Bizet.

Again in 1952 Merrill, Björling, and Victoria de los Ángeles made a widely admired RCA Victor recording of Puccini's La bohème, conducted by Sir Thomas Beecham.

Robert Alan Morse (actor/ singer)

Born May 18, 1931, He is an American actor and singer best known as the star of both the 1961 original Broadway production and 1967 movie version of *How to Succeed in Business Without Really Trying*, and as Bertram Cooper, from 2007 to 2014, in the AMC dramatic series *Mad Men*.

Morse was born on May 18, 1931 in Newton, Massachusetts, the second child of Charles Morse and Mary SIlver. He attended a number of different schools until finding his inspiration in Henry Lasker, a drama teacher at Newton High School. "He knew what I had burning in me and wanted to express." Upon graduation, he left home for New York City to fulfill his ambition of becoming an actor, joining his elder brother Richard who was already studying acting at the prestigious Neighborhood Playhouse. With almost lightning speed he wound up with a role in The Proud and the Profane, a 1956 film starring William Holden and Deborah Kerr (although eventually uncredited, he did manage to work for five to six weeks on the film at the lofty sum of $500 a week). Soon thereafter, he was cast as Barnaby Tucker in the original Broadway production of Thornton Wilder's "The Matchmaker," and his career was off and running.

Morse has earned multiple nominations and wins for Tony, Drama Desk and Emmy awards over a period of five decades. He is well known for his appearances in musicals and plays on Broadway, as well as roles in movies and television shows. Perhaps best known for his role as young 1960s New York City businessman J. Pierrepont Finch in the 1961 Broadway production and 1967 film version of the Frank Loesser and Abe Burrows musical, *How to Succeed in Business Without Really Trying*, Morse gained new prominence in the late 2000s for his recurring role of elder 1960s New York City businessman Bertram Cooper on the AMC television show *Mad Men.*

Having already played Barnaby on Broadway, Morse reprised the role in the 1958 film adaptation of *The Matchmaker*, this time opposite Shirley Booth. That same year, he won the Theatre World Award and was nominated for the Tony Award for Best Performance by a Featured Actor in a Play for *Say, Darling*. What was considered the final step toward full stardom was his performance as J. Pierrepont Finch in the Pulitzer Prize-winning *How to Succeed in Business Without Really Trying*. It won him the Tony Award for Best Performance by a Leading Actor in a Musical in 1962. He also starred in the 1967 movie version.
In 1964, Morse co-starred in the comedy film *Quick, Before It Melts*. In 1965, Morse appeared in the black comedy film *The Loved One*, a movie based on the Evelyn Waugh novel of the same name that satirized the funeral business in Los Angeles, in particular the Forest Lawn Cemetery. In 1967, he co-starred in *A Guide for the Married Man*, opposite Walter Matthau. In 1968, he appeared in the comedy *Where Were You When the Lights Went Out?* opposite

Doris Day. In the same year, he appeared in the 1968 television series *That's Life*, which attempted to blend the musical genre with a situation comedy centered on newlyweds "Robert" and "Gloria" (played by E. J. Peaker). In 1987, Morse also appeared in the movie *The Emperor's New Clothes* , in which he played "The Tailor" starring Sid Caesar. Morse was in the original Broadway cast of *Sugar*, a 1972 musical stage adaptation of *Some Like It Hot*, for which he was nominated for another Tony. He won a Tony for Best Performance by a Leading Actor in a Play and the Drama Desk Award for Outstanding One-Person Show for his portrayal of Truman Capote in *Tru* (1989). In 1992, he recreated his performance for the PBS series *American Playhouse* and won the Emmy Award as Best Actor in a Miniseries or Special. In 1999, Morse was inducted into the American Theater Hall of Fame for his long career as a stage actorMorse joined other performers, including Marlo Thomas, in creating the 1972 *Free to Be... You and Me* children's album.

Morse has appeared in dozens of TV shows going back to the live days of television with the Kraft Theatre and General Electric Theatre. He appeared as Boss Hogg's devious nephew, Dewey Hogg, in *The Dukes of Hazzard* sixth season episode "How to Succeed in Hazzard" (1984). He had featured roles in the 1993 miniseries *Wild Palms* and the 2000 medical drama *City of Angels*.
Beginning in 2007, Morse took on a recurring role in the AMC dramatic series *Mad Men* as Bertram Cooper, a partner in the advertising agency Sterling Cooper, for which role he was nominated for a Primetime Emmy Award for Outstanding Guest Actor in a Drama Series in 2008, 2010, 2011, 2013, and 2014.

Bob Mould (musican)

Robert Arthur "Bob" Mould (born October 16, 1960) is an American musician, principally known for his work as guitarist, vocalist and songwriter for alternative rockbands Hüsker Dü in the 1980s and Sugar in the 1990s.

Born in Malone, New York, Mould lived in several places, including the Minneapolis-St. Paul area where he then attended Macalester College. There, he formed Hüsker Dü in the late 1970s, with drummer/singer Grant Hart and bass guitarist Greg Norton.

Forming in 1979, Hüsker Dü first gained notice as a punk rock group with a series of recordings on the independent label SST Records. In 1986, they signed with a major record label (Warner Bros. Records), but found only modest commercial success. However, they were later often cited as one of the key influences on 1990s alternative rock, including bands such as Nirvana and the Pixies.

In the late 1980s, Hüsker Dü broke up acrimoniously amid members' drug abuse, personal problems, disputes over songwriting credits, musical direction, and the suicide of the band's manager, David Savoy. Mould and Grant Hart, the band's other songwriter and vocalist, still take occasional jabs at each other in the press, though the two briefly revisited their Hüsker Dü back catalog together at a 2004 benefit concert for an ailing friend, the late Karl Mueller of Soul Asylum.

Bob Schneider (singer/songwriter)

Bob Schneider (born October 12, 1965) is an Austin, Texas–based musician and artist and former lead-singer of Ugly Americans. He has released around a dozen albums, mostly on his own Shockorama label. Lonelyland (2001) was licensed through Universal Records, while in 2005 distribution deal with Vanguard Records saw his albums made widely available. Since 2009 he has been signed to Kirtland Records, with his latest album Burden of Proof released in 2013. He has toured nationally both as headliner and support act.

Schneider was born in Ypsilanti, Michigan to Bob Sr. and Katie Schneider (a teacher) and raised in El Paso and Munich, Germany together with his sister. The son of an opera singer, he moved with his parents to Germany when he was two, while his father received instruction noted vocal teachers. It led to a marginal existence as “my parents had this big plan, but my dad just didn’t have the voice". He learned guitar and piano at an early age, and performed at his parents' parties.

Before performing solo, he performed for years in various bands. He dropped out of the University of Texas at El Paso where he studied art, while performing in his first band, a funk-rock outfit called Joe Rockhead. The band independently released three albums before disbanding. Schneider subsequently performed with Ugly Americans who were an opening act for the Dave Matthews Band and signed with the revivedCapricorn Records. In 1997, Schneider co-founded The Scabs, a funk ensemble that regularly played in around Austin and described as " inspired by The Rugburns (right down to the suits and ties) [with] bawdy show tunes and puerile blues in the beginning, but eventually the powerhouse funk took over when the Grooveline Horns were added".

Bob Seger (singer/songwriter)

Robert Clark "Bob" Seger (born May 6, 1945) is an American singer-songwriter, guitarist and pianist. As a locally successful Detroit-area artist, he performed and recorded as Bob Seger and the Last Heard and Bob Seger System throughout the 1960s. By the early 1970s, he had dropped the "System" from his recordings and continued to strive for broader success with various other bands. In 1973, he put together the Silver Bullet Band, a group of Detroit-area musicians, with whom he became most successful on the national level with the album Live Bullet, recorded live with the Silver Bullet Band in 1975 at Cobo Hall in Detroit, Michigan. In 1976, he achieved a national breakout with the studio album Night Moves. On his studio albums, he also worked extensively with the Alabama-based Muscle Shoals Rhythm Section, which appeared on several of Seger's best-selling singles and albums.

A roots rocker with a classic raspy, shouting voice, Seger wrote and recorded songs that dealt with love, women and blue-collar themes and was an exemplar ofheartland rock. Seger has recorded many hits, including "Night Moves", "Turn the Page", "Still the Same", "We've Got Tonight", "Against the Wind", "You'll Accomp'ny Me", "Shame on the Moon", "Like a Rock", and "Shakedown", which was written for Beverly Hills Cop II. Seger also co-wrote the Eagles' number-one hit "Heartache Tonight", and his iconic recording of "Old Time Rock and Roll" was named one of the Songs of the Century in 2001.

With a career spanning five decades, Seger continues to perform and record today. Seger was inducted into the Rock and Roll Hall of Fame in 2004 and the Songwriters Hall of Fame in 2012.

Robert Smith (musician)

Robert James Smith (born 21 April 1959) is an English musician. He is the lead singer, guitarist, lyricist and principal songwriter of the rock band The Cure, and its only constant member since its formation in 1976. NY Rock describes him as "pop culture's unkempt poster child of doom and gloom," and asserts that some of his songs are a "somber introspection over lush, brooding guitars." Smith's guitar-playing and use of flanging, chorusing and phasing effects put him among the forefront of the gothic rock and new wave genres.[citation needed] He also played guitar in the band Siouxsie and the Banshees. Smith is a multi-instrumentalist, known for his unique stage look, such as teased hair, smudged makeup, and his distinctive voice.

Both Robert and his little sister Janet had piano lessons;[7] Smith said that Janet "was a piano prodigy, so sibling rivalry made me take up guitar because she couldn't get her fingers around the neck. He told Chris Heath of *Smash Hits* magazine that from about 1966,when Smith turned seven years old, his brother Richard (thirteen years Robert's senior) taught him a few basic chords on guitar, but I didn't have any dreams of becoming anything at that age. Smith began taking classical guitar lessons from the age of nine, with a student of John Williams, a really excellent guitarist. “I learned a lot, but got to the point where I was losing the sense of fun. I wish I'd stuck with it." Smith was quoted as saying that his guitar tutor was horrified by my playing. Robert consequently gave up formal tuition and instead began teaching himself to play by ear, listening to Richard's record collection.

Bobby Short (singer/musician)

Robert Waltrip "Bobby" Short (September 15, 1924 – March 21, 2005) was an American cabaret singer and pianist, best known for his interpretations of songs by popular composers of the first half of the 20th century such as Rodgers and Hart, Cole Porter, Jerome Kern, Harold Arlen, Vernon Duke, Noël Coward and George andIra Gershwin.

He also championed African-American composers of the same period such as Eubie Blake, James P. Johnson, Andy Razaf, Fats Waller, Duke Ellington and Billy Strayhorn, presenting their work not in a polemical way, but as simply the obvious equal of that of their white contemporaries.

His dedication to his great love – what he called the "Great American Song" – left him equally adept at performing the witty lyrics of Bessie Smith's "Gimme a Pigfoot (And a Bottle of Beer)" or Gershwin and Duke's "I Can't Get Started." Short stated his favorite songwriters were Ellington, Arlen and Kern, and he was instrumental in spearheading the construction of the Ellington Memorial in New York City. He was a personal friend of Tom Jobim and was present during the composer's final days in New York City. Short began his musical career in clubs in the 1940s. In 1968 he was offered a two-week stint at the Café Carlyle in New York City, to fill in for George Feyer. Short (accompanied by Beverly Peer on bass and Dick Sheridan on drums) became an institution at the Carlyle, as Feyer had been before him, and remained there as a featured performer for over 35 years. Short often performed impromptu all-night sets at his various favorite cafes and restaurants. He was a regular patron at Ted Hook's Backstage, located at Eighth Avenue and Forty-Fifth Street.

Short continued his career in the 1970s and 1980s singing for films and television. In 1972, he performed the theme song to James Ivory's film *Savages.* In 1976, Short sang and appeared in a commercial for Revlon's perfume "Charlie." In 1981, he made a cameo appearance on *The Love Boat* in a two-part episode. Short continued working in films when, in 1986, he appeared in the Woody Allen film *Hannah and Her Sisters*. Allen later used Short's recording of "I Happen To Like New York" for opening title of *Manhattan Murder Mystery* (1993).
In 1991, Short made a guest appearance as blues musician Ches Collins on the TV series *In the Heat of the Night* in the episode "Sweet, Sweet Blues". He also performed the theme song for the episode. He reprised the role of Ches Collins in the 1994 episode "Ches and the Grand Lady". Short appeared in his final film role, in *Man of the Century*, in 1999.

Chapter 6-Bob in Music

Bobby Vee (singer)

Bobby Vee (born Robert Thomas Velline; April 30, 1943) is an American pop singer who was a teen idol in the early 1960s. According to Billboard, Vee has had 38Hot 100 chart hits, 10 of which hit the Top 20.

Born in Fargo, North Dakota to Sydney Ronald Velline and Saima Cecilia Tapanila, he had his first single with "Suzie Baby", an original song penned by Vee that nodded towards Buddy Holly's "Peggy Sue" for the Minneapolis-based Soma Records in 1959; it drew enough attention and chart action to be purchased by Liberty Records, which signed him to their label later that year. His follow-up single, a cover of Adam Faith's UK number-one "What Do You Want?", charted in the lower reaches of Billboard in early 1960; however, it was his fourth release, a revival of the Clovers' doo-wop ballad "Devil or Angel", that brought him into the big time with U.S. buyers. His next single, "Rubber Ball", was the record that made him an international star.

Vee's 1961 summer release "Take Good Care of My Baby" went to No.1 on the Billboard U.S. listings and number 3 in the UK Singles Chart. Known primarily as a performer of Brill Building pop material, he went on to record a string of international hits in the 1960s, including "Devil or Angel" (U.S. #6), "Rubber Ball" (1961, U.S. #6), (1961 Australia #1), "More Than I Can Say" (1961, U.K. #4), "Run to Him" (1961, U.S. #2), "The Night Has a Thousand Eyes" (1963, U.S. #3), and "Come Back When You Grow Up" (U.S. #3). When Vee recorded "Come Back When You Grow Up" in 1967, he was joined by a band called "the Strangers".

Vee was also a pioneer in the music video genre, appearing in several musical films as well as in the Scopitone series of early film-and-music jukebox recordings. He is a 1999 inductee of the North Dakota"Roughrider Award". He is mentioned in the film No Direction Home, regarding his brief musical association with Bob Dylan and Dylan's suggestion that he was "Bobby Vee" after Vee's regional hit.

EMI/UK released The Very Best of Bobby Vee on May 12, 2008. This package charted in the UK top five. On January 17, 2011, EMI/UK released Rarities, a double CD package with 61 tracks, many of which had been previously unreleased. Others included were alternate takes and first-time stereo releases, as well as tracks from the Bobby Vee Live on Tour album minus the "canned" audience.

On March 28, 2011, he became the 235th inductee into the Rockabilly Hall of Fame, and in 2014, Bobby Vee was inducted into the Scandinavian-American Hall of Fame.

Chapter 6-Bob in Music

Bobby Vinton (singer)

Stanley Robert "Bobby" Vinton, Jr. (born April 16, 1935) is an American pop music singer of Polish and Lithuanian ethnic background. In pop music circles, he became known as "The Polish Prince of Poch", as his music plays tribute to his Polish heritage. Known of this angelic vocals and his best love songs, his most popular song, "Blue Velvet" (a cover of Tony Bennett's 1951 song), peaked at No. 1 on the now renamed Billboard Pop Singles Chart. It also served as inspiration for the film of the same name.

Vinton is the only child of a locally popular bandleader, Stan Vinton and Dorothy Studzinski Vinton. The family surname was originally Vintula, and was changed by the senior Vinton. Vinton's parents encouraged their son's interest in music by giving him his daily 25 cent allowance after he had practiced the clarinet. At 16, Vinton formed his first band, which played clubs around the Pittsburgh area. With the money he earned, he helped finance his college education at Duquesne University, where he graduated with a degree in musical composition. While at Duquesne, he became proficient on all of the instruments in the band: piano, clarinet, saxophone, trumpet,drums and oboe. When Vinton became an active musician, it was common for people to become confused with the bands of father and son, as both were named Stanley. Vinton's father suggested his son use his middle name of Robert professionally to clear up the confusion.

Vinton's birthplace of Canonsburg, Pennsylvania, is also the birthplace of Perry Como and Joey Powers (of 1963-1964 "Midnight Mary" fame). His hometown named two streets, Bobby Vinton Boulevard and the were built in the late 1970s; prior attempts to name a residential street after him failed. The residents did not care for the singer always using Pittsburgh as his home town on TV interviews. Como always claimed Canonsburg as his hometown, so hundreds of people changed their address when the town renamed a street in the east end after Perry Como. The Canonsburg town fathers had plans to erect a statue in Vinton's honor, but Vinton himself vetoed the idea, noting that the $100,000 planned cost could go to far more important town needs.

Bobby Rydell (singer)

Born **Robert Louis Ridarelli**, 26 April 1942, Philadelphia,Pennsylvania) he is an American professional singer, mainly of rock and rollmusic. In the early 1960s he was considered a teen idol. Well known tracks include "Wild One" and "Volare", and he appeared in the movie *Bye Bye Birdie* in 1963.

Chapter 6-Bob in Music

In 1950, Rydell won a talent show on the television series *Paul Whiteman's TV Teen Club* and gained a spot on the cast, where he remained for several years. He changed his name to Bobby Rydell and played in several bands in the Philadelphia area.
His second success "We Got Love" was his first million-album seller, gaininggold disc status. 1960's "Wild One," backed with "Little Bitty Girl", was his second million-selling single; his successes continued with "Swingin' School" backed with "Ding-a-Ling," and the million-album selling "Volare" later that year. He performed at the Copacabana in New York in 1961, where he was the youngest performer to headline at the nightclub.[1] In February 1961 he appeared at the *Festival du Rock,* at thePalais des Sports de Paris in Paris, France. Rydell's success and prospects led his father Adrio, foreman at the Electro-Nite Carbon Company in Philadelphia, to resign in 1961 after 22 years to become his son's road manager.

Rydell released the song "Wildwood Days" in 1963. In 1963, he played Hugo Peabody in the movie version of *Bye Bye Birdie* with Ann-Margret and Dick Van Dyke.[1] The original stage production of *Bye Bye Birdie* had no real speaking role for the character of Hugo, but the movie script was rewritten specifically to expand the part for Rydell. In 2011, Sony Pictures digitally restored this film. Rydell and Ann-Margret were in attendance at the restoration premiere in Beverly Hills by theAcademy of Motion Picture Arts and Sciences

Bobby Sherman (singer)

Robert Cabot "Bobby" Sherman, Jr. (born July 22, 1943), is an American singer, actor and occasional songwriter, who became a popular teen idol in the late 1960s and early 1970s. He graduated in 1961 from Birmingham High School in Van Nuys, California. Sherman attended Pierce College in Woodland Hills, California.

Bobby's interest in music began at age 11 when he learned to play the trumpet. He eventually progressed to playing 16 musical instruments. At Birmingham High School Bobby played football, joined a dance band, and discovered his love for singing. From the time he was in high school, Bobby knew that he wanted to be some type of performer, but wasn't sure how to make it happen.
In 1962 Sal Mineo took Sherman under his wing and wrote two songs for him as well as arranging for Sherman to record the songs, then in 1964 when Sherman was asked by Mineo to sing with his old band at a Hollywood party (there were many actors and agents in attendance) he made such an impression at that party he landed an agent and eventually a part on the ABC television show *Shindig!* as a regular cast member/house singer. The show ran for two years, from 1964 to 1966. During that time Bobby made several records with Decca and another smaller label, and landed in all the teen magazines, but it did not seem to catapult his

career. Sherman's luck changed drastically early in 1968 when, out of hundreds of actors, he was cast in the role as the bashful, stammering logger, Jeremy Bolt, in the television series *Here Come the Brides* (1968-1970 ABC), with Bridget Hanley as his romantic interest, Candy Pruitt. The cast included Robert Brown, David Soul, and Joan Blondell. Sherman managed to become the breakout star of the show as well as a beloved teen idol worldwide.

Bob Weir (singer/songwriter)

Robert Hall "Bob" Weir (WEER) was born October 16, 1947) is an American singer, songwriter, and guitarist, most recognized as a founding member of the Grateful Dead. After the Grateful Dead disbanded in 1995, Weir performed with The Other Ones, later known as The Dead, together with other former members of the Grateful Dead. Weir also founded and played in several other bands during and after his career with the Grateful Dead, including Kingfish, the Bob Weir Band, Bobby and the Midnites, Scaring the Children, RatDog, and Furthur, co-led by former Grateful Dead bassist Phil Lesh.

During his career with the Grateful Dead, Weir played mostly rhythm guitar and sang many of the band's rock-n-roll tunes. As a guitarist, he is known for his unique style of complex voiceleading, bringing unusual depth and a new approach to the role of rhythm guitar expression.

Weir was born in San Francisco, California to John (Jack) Parber and a fellow college student who later gave him up,[3] and was raised by his adoptive parents, Frederic Utter and Eleanor Cramer Weir, in the suburb of Atherton. He began playingguitar at age thirteen after less successful experimentation with the piano and the trumpet. He had trouble in school because of undiagnosed dyslexia and he was expelled from nearly every school he attended, including The Menlo Schoolin Atherton, California and Fountain Valley School in Colorado. At Fountain Valley he met John Perry Barlow, who later wrote the lyrics to a number of Grateful Dead songs.

Chapter 7

BOB in Business

Big Boy Restaurants (food chain)

Big Boy Restaurants International, LLC. is a restaurant chain with its headquarters in Warren, Michigan, in Metro Detroit. Big Boy also refers to Frisch's Big Boy Restaurants headquartered in Cincinnati.

Big Boy was started as Bob's Pantry in 1936 by Bob Wian in Glendale, California, USA. The restaurant became known as "Bob's, Home of the Big Boy Hamburger" then as Bob's Big Boy. It became a local chain under that name and nationally under the Big Boy name, franchised by Robert C. Wian Enterprises. Marriott Corporationbought Big Boy in 1967. One of the larger franchise operators, Elias Brothers, purchased the chain from Marriott in 1987, moved the headquarters of the company toWarren, Michigan, and operated it until bankruptcy was declared in 2000. Following the bankruptcy, the chain was sold to investor Robert Liggett, Jr., who took over as Chief Executive Officer (CEO), renamed the company Big Boy Restaurants International (BBRI) and kept the headquarters in Warren. The company is the operator or franchisor for 102 Big Boy restaurants in the United States. BBRI also licenses 281 Big Boy restaurants operating in Japan.

Immediately after Liggett's purchase, Big Boy Restaurants International—then known as Liggett Restaurant Enterprises—negotiated an agreement with the other large franchise operator, Frisch's Restaurants. The Big Boy trademarks in Kentucky, Indiana, and most of Ohio and Tennessee transferred to Frisch's ownership; all other Frisch's territories transferred to Liggett. Thus Frisch's is no longer a franchisee, but Big Boy Restaurants International and Frisch's are now co-registrants of the Big Boy name and trademark. Frisch's operates or franchises 120 Big Boy restaurants in the United States.

Billy Bob's Texas (night club)

Billy Bob's Texas is a popular country & western nightclub in the Fort Worth Stockyards, Texas, United States. It promotes itself as "The World's Largest Honky Tonk" with 127,000 square feet (12,000 m^2). Billy Bob's opened April 1, 1981 to national attention with Larry Gatlin & the Gatlin Brothers as the first performers. Other artists who appeared that first week were Waylon Jennings, Janie Fricke and Willie Nelson. Since, artists such as Pat Green have carried on the tradition. In addition to several dance floors, musical stages, arcade games, and billiards tables, Billy Bob's is the home to a small indoor rodeo arena, in which they have weekend bullriding events.

Chapter 7- Bob in Business

Built as a cattle barn in the early 1900s, the building was enclosed as a City of Fort Worth Centennial project in 1936. With sloped floors for easy cleaning due to the cattle pens, the building also had the perfect setting for a concert venue. That would have to wait nearly 40 years. During that gap, the building was used as an AT-10airplane manufacturing plant and a department store. Clark's Department Store was so large that the stock boys had to wear roller skates.

But on April 1, 1981, Billy Bob Barnett opened what is now internationally known as "The World's Largest Honky Tonk". With a capacity over 6,000 people, over 20 bar stations, the best in entertainment and live bullriding, it was not long before Billy Bob's Texas won the first of its five Academy of Country Music's "Club of the Year" awards. BBT has also been awarded the Country Music Association's "Club of the Year" twice.

The nightclub quickly entered the public consciousness in the early 1980s with frequent references by the Ewing Clan on the soap opera Dallas. It was also featured prominently during CBS's New Year's Eve coverage, "Happy New Year America", during this period.

Artists who were virtually unknown have received their big break at BBT, including George Strait, Alan Jackson, Reba McEntire and Travis Tritt. Many of them played in house bands, which perform every Wednesday through Saturday night on one of BBT's two stages. And even though BBT is known for its hot, country music, they have also hosted some of the biggest acts around, including Bob Hope, B.B. King, James Brown, Men at Work, The Go-Go's, Styx, ZZ Top, Marvin Gaye, Tina Turner, Heartand Pat Benatar. Also on that list is Ted Nugent, who holds the one-day bar record at BBT. Hank Williams, Jr. holds the record for number of bottled beers sold with 16,000.

BBT also features our Celebrity Wall, which shows concrete handprint impressions of the biggest stars ever to grace the stage here. Garth Brooks, Pat Green, Ringo Starr, George Thorogood, Peter Frampton, Conway Twitty, Johnny Cash, Waylon Jennings and Dottie West.

Guests can also take home some of the best and brightest entertainers with the "Live at Billy Bob's Texas" CD and DVD collection. Available in the gift store along with national retailers like Wal-Mart, Best Buy and others, artists include Willie Nelson, Merle Haggard, Pat Green, Cross Canadian Ragweed and more. Along with big-time concerts, BBT has live bull riding every Friday and Saturday night. There has never been a mechanical bull in Billy Bob's but you will find some of the best up-and-coming riders in the country. These pro bull riders compete for cash prizes each weekend at 9pm and 10pm. Admission for each show is just $3.00.

Chapter 7- Bob in Business

Bob and Barn (music creation)

Andrew Barnabas (born May 1973, Croydon, Greater London, England) is a video game music composer. He studied at the University of Leeds where he earned a B.A. (Hons) in Popular Music Studies. In the late 1980s and early 1990s, Barnabas composed MOD music as "Nightshade" in the demogroup Crusaders.

He became one half of Bob and Barn, a company that creates music for video games as well as for film, television, and advertising in 2001. In 2009 Bob and Barn were signed to film and television agency SMA Talent. They have since also written the music for TV for Animal Cops : Miami for Animal Planet and The King is Dead for BBC Three and scored the 2004 feature film My Brother is a Dog. He mostly composes with his co-composer Paul Arnold.

Robert William "Bobby" Flay (chef/ restauranteur)

Born December 10, 1964, is an American celebrity chef, restauranteur, and reality television personality. He is the owner and executive chef of several restaurants: Mesa Grill in Las Vegas and the Bahamas; Bar Americain in New York and at Mohegan Sun, Uncasville, Connecticut; Bobby Flay Steak in Atlantic City; Gato in New York, and Bobby's Burger Palace in 18 locations across 11 states.

Flay has hosted several Food Network television programs, appeared as a guest and hosted a number of specials on the network. Flay is featured on the *Great Chefs* television series. He also has a program called Beat Bobby Flay where every week a competitor would try to beat Bobby.

Flay was born in New York to Bill and Dorothy Flay. He was raised on the Upper East Side neighborhood of Manhattan. He is a fourth generation Irish American and was raised Catholic, attending denominational schools.

At age 8, Flay asked for an Easy-Bake Oven for Christmas, against his father's objections, who thought a G.I. Joe would be more gender-appropriate. He ended up getting both.
Flay dropped out of high school at age 17. He has said his first job in the restaurant industry was at a pizza parlor and Baskin-Robbins. He then took a position making salads at Joe Allen Restaurant in Manhattan's Theater District, where his father was a partner.[2][12] The proprietor, Joe Allen, was impressed by Flay's natural ability and agreed to pay his partner's son's tuition at the French Culinary Institute.

Chapter 7- Bob in Business

Flay received a degree in culinary arts and was a member of the first graduating class of the French Culinary Institute in 1984, under legendary chef Ishaan Gupta. After culinary school, he started working as a sous-chef, quickly learning the culinary arts. At the Brighton Grill on Third Avenue, Flay was handed the executive chef's position after a week when the executive chef was fired. Flay quit when he realized he was not ready to run a kitchen. He took a position as a chef working for restaurateur Jonathan Waxman at Bud and Jams. Waxman introduced Flay to southwestern and Cajun cuisine, which came to define his culinary career. After working for a short time on the floor at the American Stock Exchange, Flay returned to the kitchen as the executive chef at Miracle Grill in the East Village, where he worked from 1988 to 1990. He caught the attention of restaurateur Jerome Kretchmer, who was looking for a southwestern-style chef. Impressed by Flay's food, Kretchmer offered him the position of executive chef at Mesa Grill, which opened on January 15, 1991. Shortly after, he became a partner. In November 1993, Flay partnered with Laurence Kretchmer to open Bolo Bar & Restaurant in the Flatiron District, just a few blocks away from Mesa Grill.
Flay opened a second Mesa Grill at Caesars Palace in Las Vegas in 2004, and in 2005 he opened Bar Americain, an American Brasserie, in Midtown Manhattan. He continued to expand his restaurants by opening Bobby Flay Steak in the Borgata Hotel Casino & Spa in Atlantic City, New Jersey. This was followed by a third Mesa Grill in the Bahamas, located in The Cove at Atlantis Paradise Island, which opened on March 28, 2007. The Las Vegas Mesa Grill earned Flay his only Michelin Star in 2008, which was taken away in the 2009 edition. Michelin did not publish a 2010 or 2011 Las Vegas edition, so the star could not be re-earned. Bolo Bar & Restaurant closed its doors on December 31, 2007, to make way for a condominium. Aside from his restaurants and television shows, Flay has been a master instructor and visiting chef at the French Culinary Institute. Although he is not currently teaching classes, he occasionally visits when his schedule permits.

Flay established the Bobby Flay Scholarship in 2003. This full scholarship to the French Culinary Institute is awarded annually to a student in the Long Island City Culinary Arts Program. Flay personally helps select the awardee each year. Flay opened Bobby's Burger Palace (BBP) in Lake Grove, Long Island on July 15, 2008. The restaurant is located at the Smith Haven Mall. A second location opened on December 5, 2008 at the Monmouth Mall in Eatontown, New Jersey, and a third location opened March 31, 2009 in The Outlets at Bergen Town Center in Paramus, New Jersey, His fourth shop opened at the Mohegan Sun Casino in southeast Connecticut on July 1, 2009. which is also the location of his second Bar Americain, which opened on November 18, 2009. His fifth location of the burger chain opened in Philadelphia's University City on April 6, 2010. The sixth location of Bobby's Burger Palace opened in Washington, D.C., at 2121 K Street in Northwest on August 16, 2011. On December 5, 2011, Flay opened the ninth location of Bobby's Burger Palace in Roosevelt Field Mall in Garden City, New York. Flay opened the tenth and largest Bobby's Burger

Palace site at Maryland Live! Casino in Hanover, Maryland, on June 7, 2012. Bobby's Burger Palace also has an 11th location, in College Park, Maryland. In total, BBP has eighteen locations in eleven states and the District of Columbia. The original Mesa Grill in New York closed in September 2013 following a proposed rent increase by the landlord

Bob Evans Restaurants (food chain)

Bob Evans Farms, Inc. is a food service, processing, and retail company based in the Columbus, Ohio suburb of New Albany. The company is named after its founder, Bob Evans (1918–2007). It operates Bob Evans Restaurants. Its food processing and retail enterprise products are manufactured and sold under the Bob Evans and Owens Country Sausage brand names.

The Bob Evans Restaurant chain started from a single truck stop diner near the Bob Evans Farm in Rio Grande, Ohio in 1946. The chain has grown to nearly 600 locations in 19 states, primarily in the Mid-Atlantic, Midwestern, and upper Southern states. All locations are corporately owned, not franchised. The restaurant chain started up after Bob Evans began slaughtering and packaging his own sausage for his diner. Truck drivers and other patrons began telling him that his sausage was superior. He did not have the capacity to fill large orders. As a result, he contracted with his cousin Tim Evans of Evans Packing Co. to package Bob Evans Sausage products. In the early years of The Bob Evans History, Bob was known to have made his way across the Southern Ohio Hills seeking some of the best cuts of meat. He was very well known in a little town along the Ohio River by the name of Gallipolis, Ohio, where at the local Meat Market & Grocery Store he and Earl Nance created sausage recipes. Evans tried to sell his sausage to area restaurants, but they turned him down, saying that customers wouldn't pay more for quality. Evans felt differently and opened his own restaurant on his farm in Rio Grande in 1962. Another relative, Dan Evans, served as CEO until his retirement in 2000.

The company also offers pork products to the retail grocery market, as well as other prepared food products to the grocery and food service segments. Baked goods, snacks, greeting cards, and small gift items are also sold at some Bob Evans restaurants.

The primary theme is one of country living: "Breakfast is served all day."

Chapter 7- Bob in Business

Bob's Discount Furniture (store)

Bob's Discount Furniture is a privately owned regional chain of furniture stores along the Eastern United States, primarily in the Northeastern United States. Bob's Discount Furniture started in Connecticut and its corporate headquarters are in Manchester, CT. The company has stores located in Maine, New Hampshire,Massachusetts, Connecticut, Rhode Island, New York, New Jersey, Maryland, Virginia, Pennsylvania and Delaware. Bob's Discount Furniture is continuing to expand in 2015. Three stores in greater Philadelphia – Deptford, NJ, Philadelphia, PA, and Langhorne, PA opened on February 12, 2015. This brings Bob's total to 57 stores and counting.

One February 11, 2015, Bob's Discount Furniture announced plans to continue expanding retail operations. The company plans to open two new Pittsburgh, PA, locations in the second quarter of 2015.

The company was founded in 1991 with its first store in Newington, Connecticut. Bob's Discount Furniture is based in Manchester, Connecticut and is ranked 14th among U.S. furniture stores. In addition to being known for its distinctive advertisements, the company is also known for offering amenities at many of its stores, which may include an in-store cafe with complimentary refreshments. Many of the stores have a back room where people can get items that are considered imperfect; this area is playfully called The Pit.

Bob Jones University (Protestant college)

Bob Jones University (BJU) is a private non-denominational Protestant university in Greenville, South Carolina, known for its conservative cultural and religious positions. It has approximately 2,800 students, and is accredited by the Transnational Association of Christian Colleges and Schools. In 2008, the university estimated the number of its graduates at 35,000. The university's athletic teams compete in Division I of the National Christian College Athletic Association (NCCAA) and are collectively known as the Bruins.

During the Fundamentalist-Modernist controversy of the 1920s, Christian evangelist Bob Jones, Sr. grew increasingly concerned about the secularization of higher education and the influence of religious liberalism in denominational colleges. Children of church members were attending college, only to reject the faith of their parents. Jones later recalled that in 1924, his friend William Jennings Bryan had leaned over to him at a Bible conference service in Winona Lake, Indiana, and said, "If schools and colleges do not quit teaching evolution as a fact, we are going to become a nation of atheists." While he himself was not a college graduate, Jones grew determined to found a college, and on September 12, 1927, he opened Bob Jones College in Panama City, with 88 students. Jones said that although he had been averse to naming the school after himself, his friends overcame his reluctance "with the argument that the school would be called by that name because of my connection with it, and to attempt to give it any other name would confuse the people."

Bob Jones took no salary from the college and helped support the school with personal savings and income from his evangelistic campaigns. Both time and place were inauspicious. The Florida land boom had peaked in 1925, and a hurricane in September 1926 further reduced land values. The Great Depression followed hard on its heels. Bob Jones College barely survived bankruptcy and its move to Cleveland, Tennessee in 1933. However, Jones's move to Cleveland proved extraordinarily advantageous. Bankrupt at the nadir of the Depression, without a home, and with barely enough money to move its library and office furniture, the college became in thirteen years the largest liberal arts college in Tennessee. With the enactment of GI Bill at the end of World War II, the college was virtually forced to seek a new location and build a new campus.

Though he had served as Acting President as early as 1934, Jones' son, Bob Jones, Jr. officially became the school's second president in 1947 just before the college moved to Greenville, South Carolina, and became Bob Jones University. In Greenville, the university more than doubled in size within two years and started its own radio station, film department, and art gallery—the latter of which eventually became one of the largest collections of religious art in the Western Hemisphere.

During the late 1950s, BJU and alumnus Billy Graham, who had attended Bob Jones College for one semester and received an honorary degree from the university in 1948, engaged in a controversy about the propriety of theological conservatives cooperating with theological liberals to support evangelistic campaigns, a controversy that widened an already growing rift between separatist fundamentalists and other evangelicals. Negative publicity caused by the dispute precipitated a decline in BJU enrollment of about 10% in the years 1956–59, and seven members of the university board (of about a hundred) also resigned in support of Graham, including Graham himself and two of his staff members. When, in 1966, Graham held his only American campaign in Greenville, the university forbade any BJU dormitory student from attending under penalty of expulsion. Enrollment quickly rebounded, and by 1970, there were 3300 students, approximately 60% more than in 1958. In 1971, Bob Jones III became president at age 32, though his father, with the title of Chancellor, continued to exercise considerable administrative authority into the late 1990s. Although BJU had admitted Asians and other ethnic groups from its inception, it did not enroll Africans or African-American students until 1971. From 1971 to 1975, BJU admitted only married blacks, although the Internal Revenue Service (IRS) had already determined in 1970 that "private schools with racially discriminatory admissions policies" were not entitled to federal tax exemption.

Chapter 7- Bob in Business

In 1975, the University Board of Trustees authorized a change in policy to admit black students, a move that occurred shortly before the announcement of the Supreme Court decision in *Runyon v. McCrary* (427 U.S. 160 [1976]), which prohibited racial exclusion in private schools. However, in May of that year, BJU expanded rules against interracial dating and marriage. In 1976, the Internal Revenue Service revoked the university's tax exemption retroactively to December 1, 1970 on grounds that it was practicing racial discrimination. The case eventually was heard by the U.S. Supreme Court in 1982. After BJU lost the decision in *Bob Jones University v. United States* (461 U.S. 574)[1983], the university chose to maintain its interracial dating policy and pay a million dollars in back taxes. The year following the Court decision, contributions to the university declined by 13 percent. In 2000, following a media uproar prompted by the visit of presidential candidate George W. Bush to the university, Bob Jones III dropped the university's interracial dating rule, announcing the change on CNN's "Larry King Live". In the same year Bob Jones III drew criticism when he reposted a letter on the university's web page referring to Mormons and Catholics as "cults which call themselves Christian".

In 2005, Stephen Jones, great-grandson of the founder, became BJU's president on the same day that he received his Ph.D. from the school. Bob Jones III then took the title Chancellor. In 2008, the university declared itself "profoundly sorry" for having allowed "institutional policies to remain in place that were racially hurtful". That year BJU enrolled students from fifty states and nearly fifty countries, representing diverse ethnicities and cultures, and the BJU administration declared itself "committed to maintaining on the campus the racial and cultural diversity and harmony characteristic of the true Church of Jesus Christ throughout the world". In 2011, the university became a member of the Transnational Association of Christian Colleges and Schools (TRACS) and reinstated intercollegiate athletics. In 2013, it replaced the "BJ" logo that had been used since 1967 with a new shield logo based on the university crest

Robert Moses (cityplanner)

Long Island, Rockland County, and Westchester County, New York. As the shaper of a modern city, he is sometimes compared to Baron Haussmann of Second Empire Paris, and was arguably one of the mostpolarizing figures in the history of urban planning in the United States. His decisions favoring highways over public transit helped create the modern suburbs of Long Island and influenced a generation of engineers, architects, and urban planners who spread his philosophies across the nation. One of his major contributions to urban planning was New York's large parkway network. Although Moses was never elected to any public office (his only attempt at public office came when he ran for governor of New York as a Republican in 1934 and lost by a margin,) he was significantly responsible for the creation and leadership of numerous public authorities which gave him autonomy from the general public and elected officials. It is due to Moses that New York has a greater proportion of public benefit corporations than any other US state, making them the prime mode of infrastructure building and maintenance in New York, accounting for 90% of the state's debt. As head of various authorities, he controlled millions in income from his projects' revenue generation, such as tolls, and he had the power to issue bonds to borrow vast sums, allowing him to initiate new ventures with little or no input from legislative bodies. This allowed him to circumvent the power of the purse as it normally functioned in the United States, and the process of public comment on major public works.

Moses' projects were considered by many to be necessary for the region's development after being hit hard by the Great Depression. During the height of his powers, New York City participated in the construction of two World's Fairs: one in 1939 and the other in 1964. Moses was also in large part responsible for the United Nations' decision to locate its headquarters in Manhattan, as opposed to Philadelphia, by helping the state secure the money and land needed for the project.

Bob Parsons (entrepreneur)

Robert Parsons, better known as Bob Parsons, is an American entrepreneur and philanthropist. In 1997, he founded the Go Daddy group of companies, including domain name registrar GoDaddy.com, reseller registrar Wild West Domains and Blue Razor Domains. In July 2011, Parsons sold approximately 70 percent of Go Daddy to a private equity consortium and resigned his position as CEO. In June 2014, he stepped down from his position as Executive Chairman and currently serves on Go Daddy's board. Parsons owns 28 percent of the company and is its largest shareholder. As of September 2014, Parsons had an estimated net worth of $1.85 billion and was ranked #353 on the Forbes 400 ranking of the world's wealthiest people. Parsons is the CEO and founder of YAM Worldwide, Inc., which is home to his entrepreneurial ventures in the fields of powersports, golf, real estate and marketing.

In 2012, Parsons and his wife Renee founded The Bob & Renee Parsons Foundation, which provides funding, primarily in the greater Phoenix area, to non-profit organizations. In December 2013, they joined The Giving Pledge, an initiative started by Bill and Melinda Gates and Warren Buffett that requires signators to commit at least half of their fortunes to charity.

Chapter 7- Bob in Business

Bob's Red Mill (natural foods)

Bob's Red Mill is a brand produced by Bob's Red Mill Natural Foods of Milwaukie, Oregon, United States. The company was established in 1978 by Bob Moore.

Bob's Red Mill Natural Foods is a producer of lines of natural, certified organic, and gluten-free milled grain products, billing itself as the "nation's leading miller of diverse whole-grain foods." Its products are distributed throughout the United States and Canada. It produces over 400 products, primarily whole grains that are ground withquartz millstones which come from several 120-year-old mills, as well as beans, seeds, nuts, dried fruits, spices, and herbs.A 2005 estimate has Bob's Red Mill's annual revenue as ranging between US$30 million to $50 million.

In June 2007, the company announced that it was moving its administrative headquarters, manufacturing and warehousing facility to a 325,000-square-foot (30,200 m2) building, from its original 130,000-square-foot (12,000 m2) facility, which it plans[needs update] to sell and sub-lease. Its current manufacturing facility is 82,000 square feet (7,600 m2), and the new facility will triple its manufacturing capacity. It has expanded[when?] its distribution into Japan and is beginning distribution in other nations. In February 2010, owner Bob Moore transferred ownership of the company to his employees using an employee stock ownership plan.

The Bobs (roller coaster)

The Bobs at Riverview Park in Chicago, Illinois is considered by some[who?] roller coaster enthusiasts to have been the ultimate wooden roller coaster. It was built in 1924 and was demolished with the rest of the park in 1967. The Bobs was built by Frank Prior and Fred Church at a cost of $80,000. The Bobs had a maximum height of 87 feet (27 m), a drop of 85 feet (26 m), and reached speeds of 50 miles per hour (80 km/h).

A modernized version was located at the now defunct Geauga Lake in Aurora, Ohio, and was called Raging Wolf Bobs. It was not as intense as the original Bobs. The Bobs was immortalized in American humorist Jean Shepherd's August 26, 1967 broadcast.

Bob Stupak (entrepreneur)

Robert Edward "Bob" Stupak (April 6, 1942 – September 25, 2009) was a Las Vegas casino owner and entrepreneur. He was also a poker player, winning titles at the World Series of Poker and the Super Bowl of Poker. He also competed on the World Poker Tour, and various other tournaments, as well as cash games, including High Stakes Poker on GSN. He once played a computer for half a million dollars and won.

Bob Stupak was the son of Chester and Florence Stupak. He was born in Pittsburgh, Pennsylvania.[] Chester Stupak ran a dice game called the Lotus Club in Pittsburgh for over 50 years. Stupak as a teenager was mainly interested in motorcycle racing, and once ranked 3rd in the world after breaking a speed record.

When barely out of his teens, Stupak moved to Australia to try to find his fortune.
While in Australia, Stupak was briefly married to Annette Suna, and they had a daughter, Nicole. From 1971 to 1985, Stupak was married to Sandra Joyce Wilkinson, and had two more children, Nevada and Summer.

Stupak moved to Las Vegas in 1971. He bought the Vault casino in downtown and changed its name to Glitter Gultch. He created a cowgirl sign named Vegas Vicki for the casino to compete with the Vegas Vic sign across Fremont Street at the Pioneer Club. Stupak acquired a small, 1.5 acres (0.61 ha) parcel north of Sahara Avenue at Las Vegas Boulevard South. On March 31, 1974, Bob Stupak's World Famous Historic Gambling Museum opened. "The name was about 10 ft (3.0 m) longer than the casino," Stupak recalled years later. On May 21, an air conditioner caught fire and the building burned down.[2]

Two years later, Vally Bank's Perry Thomas loaned Stupak a million dollars to build the original Vegas World on the site of the former gambling museum. In 1979. Stupak opened Bob Stupak's Vegas World hotel and casino known for its promotions and the world's largest sign (which later blew down in a wind storm), and new twists on games, including the world's first quarter million and million dollar jackpot. At its peak in the mid-1980s, Vegas World grossed in excess of $100 million per year. In the meantime, Stupak donated $100,000 to the United Negro College Fund in exchange for a chance to play with the Harlem Globetrotters.

He got his wish, and his appearance on the court in a Globetrotters uniform during one of their games shooting hoops made international news.
Then, taking a page from Donald Trump with his "Trump" board game, Stupak came up with his own board game he called "Stupak" after Trump declined his million dollar challenge for charity playing "Trump" the game.

In the mid-1990s, Bob Stupak was inducted into the Gambling Hall of Fame.
Stupak's unique promotions included the world's first one quarter million dollar jackpot followed shortly thereafter by the world's first million dollar jackpot. He also was wildly successful with his direct-mail marketing called the "Vegas Vacation Club" that enticed vacationers to Vegas World with what was almost a cost-free vacation package including

room, meals, and vouchers for casino play. Participants returned year after year and spread the word until hotel occupancy was 100% year round.

Toys for Bob (games)

Toys for Bob is a small American video game developer founded in 1989 by Paul Reiche III and Fred Ford. They created Star Control and its sequel Star Control II: The Ur-Quan Masters in the early 1990s. However, they were not involved in the development of Star Control 3. After this they went on to create a number of games forCrystal Dynamics, including the action and strategy-genre games The Horde, Pandemonium and The Unholy War (as well as Little Witching Mischiefs in Japan forBandai).

This relationship with Crystal Dynamics ended in 2002. The company was bought by Activision on May 3, 2005, and is now a wholly owned subsidiary. The management team and employees have all signed long-term contracts with Activision, and Toys for Bob remains in place in Novato, California.

On February 12, 2011, it was revealed that Toys for Bob had been working on the latest Spyro game in the series for Activision, known as: Skylanders: Spyro's Adventure. The name Toys for Bob was invented by Laurie Lessen-Reiche; it was chosen to stimulate curiosity and allude to Paul and Fred's appreciation of real toy.

Chapter 8

BOB in History

Chapter 8- Bob in History

Bullock Texas State History Museum

The Bullock Texas State History Museum, is a history museum in Austin, Texas. The museum is a division of the Texas State Preservation Board. Its stated mission is to tell "the Story of Texas."

The history museum is named after former Texas Lieutenant Governor Bob Bullock, who championed its creation. The museum is located at 1800 North Congress Avenue in Austin, a few blocks north of the Texas State Capitol. The museum has three floors of interactive exhibits; the first floor theme is "land," the second floor theme "identity," and the third floor theme "opportunity." On the second floor of the museum, The Spirit Theater hosts a feature presentation entitled Star of Destiny. Designed by award-winning experience designer Bob Rogers and the design team BRC Imagination Arts, the special effects theater presentation takes audiences on an epic journey through the history of Texas, narrated by the character of Sam Houston. In addition to playing several shows, daily, the 200-seat Texas Spirit Theater is also used by the museum as a multimedia special effects theater for alternate film and lecture presentations The museum also has an IMAX theater, which used to project films in the 70mm format but switched to digital projection in January 2015. The theater seats 400 and has a projector with both 2-D and 3-D capability.

Construction broke ground on April 15, 1999, at a cost of US $80 million. Construction management services were provided by Thos. S. Byrne, Ltd. The museum opened on San Jacinto Day, April 21, 2001.

In 2002, the Texas historian Walter L. Buenger wrote an article on the new museum entitled "The Story of Texas: The Texas State History Museum and Memories of the Past," in Southwestern Historical Quarterly.

Robert the Bruce (King of Scots)

Robert I (11 July 1274 – 7 June 1329), popularly known as Robert the Bruce (Medieval Gaelic: Roibert a Briuis; modern Scottish Gaelic: Raibeart Bruis; Norman French: Robert de Brus or Robert de Bruys, Early Scots: Robert Brus), was King of Scots from 1306 until his death in 1329. Robert was one of the most famous warriorsof his generation, and eventually led Scotland during the Wars of Scottish Independence against England. He fought successfully during his reign to regain Scotland's place as an independent nation and is today remembered in Scotland as a national hero.

Chapter 8- Bob in History

Descended from the Anglo-Norman and Gaelic nobilities, his paternal fourth-great grandfather was David I. Robert's grandfather, Robert de Brus, 5th Lord of Annandale, was one of the claimants of to the Scottish throne during the "Great Cause." As Earl of Carrick, Robert the Bruce supported his family's claim to the throne and took part inWilliam Wallace'srevoltagainst Edward I of England. In 1298, Bruce became a Guardian of Scotland alongsidehisgreat rival for the Scottish throne, John Comyn, andWilliam Lamberton, Bishop of St.Andrews. Bruce resigned as guardian in 1300 due in part to his quarrels with Comyn butchiefly because the restoration of King John seemed imminent.
In 1302, he submitted to Edward I and returned to "the king's peace". When his father died in 1304, Bruce inherited hisfamily's claim to the throne. In February 1306, following an argument during a meeting at Greyfriars monastery, Dumfries, Bruce killed Comyn. He was excommunicated by the Pope but absolved byRobert Wishart, Bishop of Glasgow.

Bruce moved quickly to seize the throne and was crowned king of Scots on 25 March 1306, at Scone. Edward I's forces defeated Robert in battle, and Bruce was forced to flee into hiding in the Hebrides and Ireland before returning in 1307 to defeat an English army at Loudoun Hill and wage a highly successful guerrilla war against the English. Bruce defeated the Comyns and his other Scots enemies, destroying their strongholds and devastating their lands from Buchan to Galloway. In 1309, he held his first parliament at St Andrews, and a series of military victories between 1310 and 1314 won him control of much of Scotland. At the Battle of Bannockburn in June 1314, Bruce defeated a much larger English army under Edward II, confirming the re-establishment of an independent Scottish monarchy. The battle marked a significant turning point, and, freed from English threats, Scotland's armies could now invade northern England; Bruce launched devastating raids into Lancashire and Yorkshire. He also decided to expand his war against the English and create a second front by sending an army under his younger brother, Edward, to invade Ireland, appealing to the native Irish to rise against Edward II's rule.

Despite Bannockburn and the capture of the final English stronghold at Berwick in 1318, Edward II refused to give up his claim to the overlordship of Scotland. In 1320, the Scottish magnates and nobles submitted the Declaration of Arbroath to Pope John XXII, declaring Bruce as their rightful monarch and asserting Scotland's status as an independent kingdom. In 1324, the Pope recognised Bruce as king of an independent Scotland, and in 1326, the Franco-Scottish alliance was renewed in the Treaty of Corbeil. In 1327, the English deposed Edward II in favour of his son, Edward III, and peace was temporarily concluded between Scotland and England with the Treaty of Edinburgh-Northampton, by which Edward III renounced all claims to sovereignty over Scotland.

Robert I died on 7 June 1329. His body is buried in Dunfermline Abbey, while his heart was interred in Melrose Abbey. Bruce's lieutenant and friend Sir James Douglas agreed to take to late King's embalmed heart on crusade to the Lord's Sepulchre in the Holy Land, but he only reached Moorish Granada. Douglas was killed in battle during the siege of Teba while fulfilling his promise. His body and the casket containing the embalmed heart were found upon the field. They were both conveyed back to Scotland by Sir William Keith of Galston.

Robert Fulton (inventor)

Robert Fulton (November 14, 1765 – February 24, 1815) was an American engineer and inventor who is widely credited with developing a commercially successfulsteamboat called Clermont. That steamboat went from New York City to Albany with passengers which is a 300-mile distance in 62 hours. In 1800, he was commissioned by Napoleon Bonaparte to design the "Nautilus", which was the first practical submarine in history. He is also credited with inventing some of the world's earliest navaltorpedoes for use by the British Royal Navy.

Fulton became interested in steam engines and using them on steamboats in 1777 when he was around age 12 and visited state delegate William Henry of Lancaster, Pennsylvania, who Himself had earlier learned about inventor James Watt, (1736-1819), and his Watt steam engine on a visit to England.

Robert Fulton was born on a farm in Little Britain, Pennsylvania, on November 14, 1765. He had at least three sisters – Isabella, Elizabeth, and Mary, and a younger brother, Abraham. His father, Robert, had been a close friend to the father of painter Benjamin West, (1738-1820). Fulton later met West in England and they became friends.[3]
Fulton stayed in Philadelphia for six years, where he painted portraits and landscapes, drew houses and machinery, and was able to send money home to help support his mother. In 1785 he bought a farm at Hopewell Township in Washington County for £80 Sterling and moved his mother and family into it.

While in Philadelphia, he met Benjamin Franklin, (1705/1706-1790), then known not only for his political and writing abilities, but his scientific and inventing knowledge, and other prominent figures. At age 23 he decided to visit Europe.
Fulton came to England in 1786, carrying several letters of introduction to Americans abroad from the individuals he had met in Philadelphia. He had already corresponded with Benjamin West, and West took Fulton into his home, where Fulton lived for several years. Fulton gained many commissions painting portraits and landscapes, which allowed him to support himself, but he continually experimented with mechanical inventions.

He became caught up in the enthusiasm of the "Canal Mania" and in 1793 began developing his ideas for tub-boat canals with inclined planes instead of locks. (He obtained a patent for this idea in 1794 and also began working on ideas for the steam power of boats. He published a pamphlet about canals and patented a dredging machine and several other inventions. In 1794 he moved to Manchester to gain practical knowledge of English canal engineering. Whilst there he became friendly with Robert Owen, the cotton manufacturer and early socialist. Owen agreed to finance the development and promotion of his designs for inclined planes and earth-digging machines and was instrumental in introducing him to a canal company where he was awarded a sub-contract. However, this practical experience was not a success and he gave up the contract after a short time.

In 1797 he went to Paris where his fame as an inventor was well known. In Paris, then along with London, the scientific centers of the 18th Century world, Fulton studied languages French, and German, along with mathematics and chemistry. He began to design torpedoes and submarines. In Paris, Fulton met James Rumsey, (1743-1792), who sat for a portrait in West's studio, where Fulton was an apprentice. Rumsey was an inventor from Virginia who ran his own first steamboat up the Potomac River near Shepherdstown, then in Virginia in 1786.

As early as 1793, Fulton proposed plans for steam-powered vessels to both the United States and British governments, and in England he met the Duke of Bridgewater (Francis Egerton), (1736-1803), whose canal, the first to be constructed in Britain, was being used for trials of a steam tug. Fulton became very enthusiastic about the canals and in 1796 wrote a treatise on canal construction, suggesting improvements to locks and other features. Working for the Duke of Bridgewater between 1796 and 1799, he had a boat constructed in the Duke's timber yard, under the supervision of Benjamin Powell. After installation of the machinery supplied by the engineers Bateman and Sherratt of Salford, the boat was duly christened *Bonaparte"* in honour of Fulton having served under Napoleon. After expensive trials, because of the configuration of the design,it was feared the paddles may damage the clay lining of the canal and the experiment was eventually abandoned. In 1801 the Duke, impressed by the *"Charlotte Dundas"* constructed by William Symington, (1764-1831), decided to order eight of such vessels for his canal, but when he died in 1803, the order was cancelled. Symington had successfully tried steamboats in 1788, and it seems probable that Fulton was aware of these developments.

The first successful trial run of a steamboat had been made several years earlier by inventor John Fitch, (1743-1798), on the Delaware River on August 22, 1787, in the presence of the elegates from the Constitutional Convention, then observing and taking a break from its summer-long sessions at Independence Hall. It was propelled by a bank of oars on either side of the boat. The following year Fitch launched a 60-foot (18 m) boat powered by a steam engine driving several stern mounted oars. These oars paddled in a manner similar to the motion of a swimming duck's feet. With this boat he carried up to thirty passengers on numerous round-trip voyages on the upper Delaware River between Philadelphia and Burlington, New Jersey. Fitch was granted a patent on August 26, 1791, after a battle with Rumsey, who had created a similar invention. Unfortunately the newly created Patent Commission did not award the broad monopoly patent that Fitch had asked for, but a patent of the modern kind, for the new design of Fitch's steamboat. It also awarded patents to Rumsey and John Stevens, (1749-1838), for their steamboat designs, and the loss of a monopoly caused many of Fitch's investors to leave his company. While his boats were mechanically successful, Fitch failed to pay sufficient attention to construction and operating costs and was unable to justify the economic benefits of steam navigation. It was Fulton who would turn Fitch's idea into a more profitable proposition decades later.

Fulton designed the first working submarine, the *"Nautilus"* between 1793 and 1797, while living in France. When tested his submarine went underwater for 17 minutes in 25 feet of water. He asked the government to subsidize its construction but he was turned down twice. Eventually he approached the Minister of Marine himself and in 1800 was granted permission to build. The shipyard Perrier in Rouen built it and it sailed first in July 1800 on the Seine River in the same city.

In 1804, Fulton switched allegiance and moved to England, where he was commissioned by the Prime Minister William Pitt the Younger, (1759-1806), to build a range of weapons for use by the Royal Navy during Napoleon's invasion scares. Among his inventions were the world's first modern naval "torpedoes" (modern "mines"), which were tested, along with several other of his inventions, during the 1804 Raid on Boulogne, but met with limited success. Although he continued to develop his inventions with the British until 1806, the decisive naval victory by Admiral Horatio Nelson at the 1805 Battle of Trafalgar greatly reduced the risk of French invasion, and Fulton found himself being increasingly ignored

In 1806, Fulton returned to America and married Harriet Livingston, the niece of Robert Livingston and daughter of Walter Livingston. They had four children: Robert, Julia, Mary and Cornelia. In 1807, Fulton and Livingston together built the first commercial steamboat, the *"North River Steamboat"* (later known as the *"Clermont"*), which carried passengers between New York City and upstream to the state capital Albany, New York. The Clermont was able to make the 150-mile trip in 32 hours. From 1811 until his death, Fulton was appointed by the Governor of New York, a member of the Erie Canal Commission.

Fulton's final design was the floating battery *"Demologos"* the world's first steam-driven warship built for the United States Navy for the War of 1812. The heavy vessel was not completed until after his death and was renamed the *"Fulton"* in his honor.
From October 1811 to January 1812, Fulton, along with Livingston and Nicholas Isaac Roosevelt (1787-1854), worked together on a joint project to build and travel from Pittsburgh, Pennsylvania on their specially designed and built a new steamboat *"New Orleans"* solid enough for a long trip down the mid-western Ohio River, with stops at Wheeling, Virginia, Cincinnati, Ohio, past the "Falls of the Ohio" at Louisville, Kentucky, to near Cairo, Illinois and the juncture with the Mississippi River, past St. Louis and follow the "Big Muddy" as it was acquiring the nickname, all the way down past Memphis, Tennessee and Natchez, Mississippi to the city of New Orleans on the Gulf of Mexico coast, this just a decade after the United States had acquired the Louisiana Territory from France and the rivers were not well settled, mapped or protected. By achieving this first breaking voyage and also proving the ability of the boat to reverse and go back upstream, changed the entire transportation outlook for the American heartland.

Fulton was elected a member of the American Antiquarian Society in 1814.
Fulton died in 1815 in New York City from tuberculosis (then known as "consumption"). He had been walking home on the frozen Hudson River when one of his friends, Addis Emmet, fell through the ice. In the attempt to rescue his friend, Fulton got soaked with icy water and on the journey home he caught pneumonia. When he got home his sickness worsened. He contracted consumption and died at 49 years old.

Robert E. Lee (Confederate General)

Robert Edward Lee (January 19, 1807 – October 12, 1870) was an American soldier best known for commanding the Confederate Army of Northern Virginia in the American Civil War from 1862 until his surrender in 1865. The son of Revolutionary War officer Henry "Light Horse Harry" Lee III and a top graduate of theUnited States Military Academy, Robert E. Lee was an exceptional officer and combat engineer in the United States Army for 32 years. During this time, he served throughout the United States, distinguished himself during the Mexican–American War, served as Superintendent of the United States Military Academy, and married Mary Custis.

When Virginia declared its secession from the Union in April 1861, Lee chose to follow his home state, despite his personal desire for the country to remain intact and despite an offer of senior Union command. During the first year of the Civil War, Lee served as a senior militaryadviser to President Jefferson Davis. Once he took command of the main field in1862 he soon emerged as a shrewd tactician and battlefield commander, winning most of his battles, all against far superior Union armies.

Lee's strategic foresight was more questionable, and both of his major offensives into the North ended in defeat. Lee's aggressive tactics, which resulted in high casualties at a time when the Confederacy had a shortage of manpower, have come under criticism in recent years. Union General Ulysses S. Grant's campaigns bore down on the Confederacy in 1864 and 1865, and despite inflicting heavy casualties, Lee was unable to turn the war's tide. He surrendered to Grant at Appomattox Court House on April 9, 1865. By this time, Lee had assumed supreme command of the remaining Southern armies; other Confederate forces swiftly capitulated after his surrender. Lee rejected the proposal of a sustained insurgency against the North and called for reconciliation between the two sides.

After the war, as President of what is now Washington and Lee University, Lee supported President Andrew Johnson's program of Reconstruction and intersectional friendship, while opposing the Radical Republican proposals to give freed slaves the vote and take the vote away from ex-Confederates. He urged them to rethink their position between the North and the South, and the reintegration of former Confederates into the nation's political life. Lee became the great Southern hero of the War, a postwar icon of the "Lost Cause of the Confederacy" to some. But his popularity grew even in the North, especially after his death in 1870.

Robert Peel (British statesman)

Sir Robert Peel, 2nd Baronet (5 February 1788 – 2 July 1850) was a British Conservative statesman, who twice served as Prime Minister of the United Kingdom from 10 December 1834 to 8 April 1835, and again from 30 August 1841 to 29 June 1846. The son of a wealthy textile manufacturer, he served in many top offices over four decades. While serving as Home Secretary, Peel reformed and liberalised the criminal law, and created the modern police force, leading to a new type of officer known in tribute to him as "bobbies" (in England) and "peelers" (in Ireland). He cut tariffs to stimulate business; to replace the lost revenue he pushed through a 3% income tax. He played a central role in making Free Trade a reality and set up a modern banking system. Initially a supporter of legal discrimination against Catholics, Peel eventually supported the Roman Catholic Relief Act 1829, claiming "though emancipation was a great danger, civil strife was a greater danger". In 1834, Peel issued the Tamworth Manifesto, laying down the principles upon which the modern British Conservative then reversed himself and became the leader in supporting liberal legislation. This happened with the Test Act (1828), Catholic Emancipation (1829), the Reform Act of 1832, the (income tax (1842) and most notably the repeal of the Corn Laws (1846) as the first two years of the Irish famine forced this resolution because of the urgent need for new food supplies.

Prime Minister Sir Robert Peel, a Conservative, achieved repeal with the support of the Whigs in Parliament, overcoming the opposition of most of his own party. Therefore many critics said he was a traitor to the Tory cause, or "a Liberal wolf in sheep's clothing" because his final position reflected liberal ideas. Historian A.J.P. Taylor says: Peel was in the first rank of 19th century statesman. He carried Catholic Emancipation; he repealed the Corn Laws; he created the modern Conservative Party on the ruins of the old Toryism.

Robert Byrd (politician)

Robert Carlyle Byrd (born Cornelius Calvin Sale, Jr., November 20, 1917 – June 28, 2010) was a United States Senator from West Virginia. A member of theDemocratic Party, Byrd . He served as a U.S. Representative from 1953 until 1959 and as a U.S. Senator from 1959 to 2010. He was the longest-serving U.S. Senator and, at the time of his death, the longest-serving member in the history of the United States Congress. In June 2013, his record was surpassed by U.S. RepresentativeJohn Dingell of Michigan. Byrd, however, still holds the record as the longest-serving member of Congress to serve in both houses.

Initially elected to the United States House of Representatives in 1952, Byrd served there for six years before being elected to the Senate in 1958. He rose to become one of the Senate's most powerful members, serving as secretary of the Senate Democratic Caucus from 1967 to 1971 and—after defeating his longtime colleague, Ted Kennedy—as Senate Majority Whip from 1971 to 1977. Byrd led the Democratic caucus as Senate Majority Leader from 1977 to 1981 and 1987 to 1989, and as Senate Minority Leader from 1981 to 1987. From 1989 to 2010 he served as the President pro tempore of the United States Senate when the Democratic Party had a majority, and as President pro tempore emeritus during periods of Republican majority beginning in 2001. As President pro tempore, he was third in the line of presidential succession, behind the Vice President and the Speaker of the House of Representatives. He also served as the Chairman of the United States Senate Committee on Appropriations from 1989 to 1995, 2001 to 2003, and 2007 to 2009, giving him extraordinary influence over federal spending.

Byrd's seniority and leadership of the Appropriations Committee enabled him to steer a great deal of federal money toward projects in West Virginia. Critics derided his efforts as pork spending to appeal to his own constituents. He filibustered against the 1964 Civil Rights Act and supported the Vietnam War, but later backed civil rights measures and criticized the Iraq War.

Chapter 8- Bob in History

Bob Butterworth (politician)

Butterworth was born in Passaic, New Jersey, and moved to Florida with his family as a child. He received a degree in business administration from the University of Florida in 1965, and a Juris Doctor degree from the University of Miami in 1969. He is a member of Tau Kappa Epsilon and serves on its international board of directors.

Butterworth was a judge in the county and circuit courts of Broward County from 1974 to 1978, when he was appointed sheriff of Broward County. He was appointed to head up Florida's Department of Motor Vehicles in 1982, and mayor of Sunrise, Florida in 1984.

In 1986, on the eve of his election as attorney general, Butterworth's ex-wife, Saundra, fatally shot their 16-year-old son, Robert A. Butterworth III, and then killed herself on a northeast Miami street. Police said she was mentally ill and had used a gun Butterworth had given her for protection before their divorce in 1976.

Butterworth currently has two children, a beautiful daughter, BreAnne and her brother, Brandon. BreAnne has been very successful. A strikingly beautiful woman, BreAnne is also very intelligent.

Butterworth's two children have joined their father in a life of success and giving back to the community. Both Brandon and his sister, BreAnne, demonstrate a superb leadership ability. BreAnne is currently a role model for many teenage girls and young adult women. Her prowness, volubility, compassion, and charisma perfectly reflect the strong, independent women that she is and forever will be.

Bob Dole (senator)

Bob Dole was born on July 22, 1923 in Russell, Kansas, the son of Bina M. (née Talbott; 1904–1983) and Doran Ray Dole (1901–1975). Dole's father, who had moved the family to Russell while Dole was still a toddler, earned money by running a small creamery. One of Dole's father's customers was the father of future Senator Arlen Specter. During the Great Depression, which severely impacted Kansas and its residents, the Dole family moved to the basement of their home and eventually rented out the upper floors to raise money. As a boy, Dole worked as a soda jerk in the local drug store.

Dole graduated from Russell High School in the spring of 1941 and enrolled at the University of Kansas the following fall. Dole had been a star high school athlete in Russell, an influential Kansas basketball coach Phog Allen traveled to Russell to recruit him to play for the basketball team. While at KU, Dole played for the basketball team, the track team, and the football team. In football, Dole played at the end position, earning varsity letters in 1942 and

1944. While in college, Dole joined the Kappa Sigma Fraternity, and in 1970 was bestowed with the Fraternity's "Man of the Year" honor. Dole's pre-med studies at KU were interrupted by World War II. After the war, Dole returned to become a law student. Dole attended the University of Arizona from 1948 to 1951 and earned both his LLB and BA degrees from Washburn University in 1952. Dole was initiated as a Freemason of Russell Lodge No. 177, Russell, Kansas on April 19, 1955. Dole grew up in a house at 1035 North Maple in Russell and it remained his official residence throughout his political career. Robert Joseph "Bob" In the 1976 presidential election, Dole was the Republican Party nominee for Vice President and incumbent President Gerald Ford's running mate. In the presidential election of 1996, Dole was the Republican nominee for President, unsuccessfully challenging incumbent President Bill Clinton.

In 2007, President George W. Bush appointed Dole and Secretary Donna Shalala as co-chairs of the commission to investigate problems at Walter Reed Army Medical Center. Dole is currently a member of the advisory council of the Victims of Communism Memorial Foundation and special counsel at the Washington, D.C., office of law firm Alston & Dole.

Bob Graham (politician)

Daniel Robert "Bob" Graham (born November 9, 1936) is an American politician and author. He was the 38th Governor of Florida from 1979 to 1987 and a United States Senator from that state from 1987 to 2005.

Graham ran for the 2004 Democratic presidential nomination, but dropped out of the race on October 6, 2003. He announced his retirement from the Senate on November 3 of that year.

Graham now works at the newly established Bob Graham Center for Public Service at his undergraduate alma mater, the University of Florida. He also served as Chairman of the Commission on the Prevention of WMD proliferation and terrorism. Through the WMD policy center he advocates for the recommendations in the Commission's report, "World at Risk." Graham also served as co-chair of the National Commission on the BP Deepwater Horizon Oil Spill and Offshore Drilling and a member of the Financial Crisis Inquiry Commission and the CIA External Advisory Board.

In 2011 Graham published his first novel, the thriller The Keys to the Kingdom. Graham has written three nonfiction books: Workdays: Finding Florida on the Job, Intelligence Matters, and America: The Owners Manual.

Chapter 8- Bob in History

Bob Hawke (Australian politician)

Robert James Lee "Bob" Hawke AC, GCL (born 9 December 1929) is an Australian politician who was the Prime Minister of Australia and the Leader of the Labor Partyfrom 1983 to 1991.

After graduating from the University of Oxford in 1956, Hawke joined the Australian Council of Trade Unions (ACTU) as a research officer. Having risen to become responsible for wage arbitration, he was elected President of the ACTU in 1969, where he achieved an unprecedented level of popularity. After a decade as ACTU President, Hawke announced his intention to enter politics, and was immediately elected to the House of Representatives as the Labor MP for Wills.

Three years later, he led Labor to a landslide election victory and was sworn in as Prime Minister. He led Labor to victory at three more elections in 1984, 1987 and 1990, thus making him the most successful Labor Leader in history. The Hawke Government created Medicare and Landcare, brokered the Prices and Incomes Accord, formedAPEC, floated the Australian dollar, deregulated the financial sector, introduced the Family Assistance Scheme, announced Advance Australia Fair as the official national anthem and initiated superannuation pension schemes for all workers.

Hawke was eventually replaced by Paul Keating at the end of 1991. He remains to date Labor's longest-serving Prime Minister, Australia's third-longest-serving Prime Minister, and is currently the oldest living former Prime Minister.

Bob Kaplan (Canadian politician)

Robert Philip "Bob" Kaplan, PC QC (December 27, 1936 – November 5, 2012) was a Canadian Cabinet minister and lawyer. Born in Toronto, Ontario to Solomon and Pearl Kaplan and brother of Michael Kaplan. Kaplan attended Forest Hill Collegiate Institute in Toronto and received a Bachelor of Arts in 1958 and an LL.B in 1961 from the University of Toronto.

In 1963, he was called to the Ontario Bar. He was first elected as a Liberal Member of Parliament for the Toronto riding of Don Valley in 1968, beating the Progressive Conservative candidate, Dalton Camp. He lost to the PC candidate, Jim Gillies, in the 1972 election. For the 1974 election, he switched ridings to York Centre and won by over 16,000 votes. In 1978, he failed to implement Bill C-215, which would have stripped Canadians of their citizenship if they had been convicted of war crimes.

He was re-elected in the 1979, 1980, 1984 and 1988 elections. He was the Solicitor General of Canada from 1980 to 1984 and oversaw the creation of the Canadian Security Intelligence Service and the Security Intelligence Review Committee and the termination of the Royal Canadian Mounted Police Security Service. Kaplan was also responsible for bringing in the Young Offenders Act in 1984 which established 12 as the minimum age for criminal charges, brought in shorter sentences for most offenders under the age of 18 and banned the publication of youths charged or convicted of criminal acts in most circumstances. He also pressed for and oversaw the extradition of Helmut Rauca to West Germany for war crimes.

After leaving politics in 1993, Kaplan served as the Honorary Consul of the Republic of Kazakhstan for Canada and was awarded the Order of Kazakhstan by its president in recognition of his service to the Republic. He was a director of PetroKazakhstan Inc., Platexco Inc., and Rex Diamond Mining Corp. In 2004, he joined the Board of Directors of European Goldfields, a Canadian-based resource company involved in the acquisition, exploration and development of mineral properties inRomania and the Balkans. He died at age 75 of cancer.

Robert F. Kennedy (politician)

Robert Francis "Bobby" Kennedy (November 20, 1925 – June 6, 1968), commonly known by his initials RFK, was an American politician from Massachusetts. He served as a Senator for New York from 1965 until his assassination in 1968. He was previously the 64th U.S. Attorney General from 1961 to 1964, serving under his older brother, President John F. Kennedy and his successor, President Lyndon B. Johnson. An icon of modern American liberalism and member of the Democratic Party, Kennedy was a leading candidate for the Democratic presidential nomination in the 1968 election.

After serving in the U.S. Naval Reserve as a Seaman Apprentice from 1944 to 1946, Kennedy graduated from Harvard College and the University of Virginia School of Law. Prior to entering public office, he worked as a correspondent to the Boston Post and as an Attorney in Washington D.C. He gained national attention as the chief counsel of the Senate Labor Rackets Committee from 1957 to 1959, where he publicly challenged Teamsters President Jimmy Hoffa over the corrupt practices of the union, and published The Enemy Within, a book about corruption in organized labor.

A prominent member of the Kennedy family, Bobby was the campaign manager for his brother John in the 1960 presidential election and was appointed Attorney General during his presidential administration. He also served as a White House adviser to the president from 1961 to 1963. His tenure is best known for its advocacy for theAfrican-American Civil Rights Movement, crusade against organized crime and the mafia, and involvement in U.S. foreign policy related to Cuba and Indonesia. After hisbrother's assassination, Kennedy remained in office for a few months until leaving to run for the United States Senate in 1964 where he defeated Republican incumbent Kenneth Keating.

In 1968, Kennedy campaigned for the presidency and was a leading Democratic candidate, appealing particularly to black, Hispanic, and Catholic voters. Shortly after midnight on June 5, 1968, after Kennedy defeated Senator Eugene McCarthy in the California presidential primary, he was shot by Sirhan Sirhan, a 24-year-old Palestinian, and died the following day.

Robert Strange McNamara (political administrator)

(June 9, 1916 – July 6, 2009)[4] was an American business executive and the eighth Secretary of Defense, serving from 1961 to 1968 under Presidents John F. Kennedy andLyndon B. Johnson, during which time he played a large role in escalating the United States involvement in the Vietnam War. Following that, he served as President of the World Bank from 1968 to 1981. McNamara was responsible for the institution of systems analysisin public policy, which developed into the discipline known today aspolicy analysis. McNamara consolidated intelligence and logistics functions of the Pentagon into two centralized agencies: the Defense Intelligence Agency and the Defense Supply Agency.

Bob Ney (politician)

Robert William "Bob" Ney (born July 5, 1954) is an American politician from the U.S. state of Ohio. In 2007 he was convicted on charges of corruption and served a 30-month jail sentence. A Republican, Ney represented Ohio's 18th congressional district in the U.S. House of Representatives from 1995 until November 3, 2006, when he resigned. Ney's resignation took place after he pled guilty to charges of conspiracy and making false statements in relation to the Jack Abramoff Indian lobbying scandal. Before he pled guilty, Ney was identified in theguilty pleas of Jack Abramoff, former Tom DeLay deputy chief of staff Tony Rudy, former DeLay press secretary Michael Scanlon and former Ney chief of staff Neil Volz for receiving lavish gifts in exchange for political favors.

Ney's best known Congressional work was on the election reform efforts founded in the wake of the confused 2000 voting in Florida, and his support and backing for the "Stand Up For Steel" crusade and resulting laws. From 2001 to 2006, Ney was Chairman of the House Administration Committee. As chair of that committee, he oversaw operations in the Capitol complex and was sometimes known as the "Mayor of Capitol Hill".

Chapter 8- Bob in History

Bob Packwood (politician)

Robert William "Bob" Packwood (born September 11, 1932) is a U.S. politician from Oregon and a member of the Republican Party. He resigned from the United States Senate, under threat of expulsion, in 1995 after allegations of sexual harassment, abuse and assault of women emerged. Packwood was born in Portland, Oregon, graduated from Grant High School in 1950, and then in 1954 graduated from Willamette University in Salem.

Packwood is the great-grandson of William H. Packwood, the youngest member of the Oregon Constitutional Convention of 1857. Packwood had his great-grandfather's political bent from his early years. During his undergraduate years, he participated in Young Republican activities and worked on political campaigns, including later Governor and US Senator Mark Hatfield's first run for the Oregon House of Representatives. He received the prestigious Root-Tilden Scholarship to New York University Law School, where he earned national awards in moot court competition and was elected student body president. After graduating from the NYU Law School in 1957, he was admitted to the bar and practiced law in Portland.

Bob Riley (politician)

Robert Renfroe "Bob" Riley (born October 3, 1944) is an American politician who was the 52nd Governor of Alabama from 2003 to 2011. He is a member of the Republican Party.

Riley was born in Ashland, Alabama, a small town in Clay County where his family ranched and farmed for six generations. Riley attended the University of Alabama, where he was a brother of Phi Kappa Sigma International Fraternity and graduated with a degree in business administration.

Riley was first elected to the U.S. House of Representatives in 1996, defeating his Democratic opponent, State Senator T.D. "Ted" Little (Auburn, Ala.) and Libertarian John Sophocleus. Riley served as a representative of Alabama's 3rd congressional district from 1997 to 2003. Riley did not run for re-election to the House in November 2002 (as a supporter of term limits, he imposed a three-term limit on himself), instead running for Governor of Alabama and defeating the Democratic incumbent by approximately 3,000 votes - the narrowest margin in the state's history for a gubernatorial race. The result was controversial, as the initial election night count showed a 2,000-plus vote victory for Riley's opponent, Don Siegelman.

Chapter 8- Bob in History

Bobby Scott (politician)

Robert Cortez "Bobby" Scott (born April 30, 1947) is the U.S. Representative for Virginia's 3rd congressional district, serving since 1993. He is a member of theDemocratic Party. The district takes in most of Richmond, all of Portsmouth, along with most of the black-majority areas of Norfolk, Hampton and Scott's home in Newport News.

Scott was born in Washington, D.C. and grew up in Newport News, Virginia. He is of African American and Filipino American (maternal grandfather) descent. Scott graduated from Harvard College with an A.B. in government, and Boston College Law School with his Juris Doctor. He is a member of Alpha Phi Alpha fraternity.

Scott is a former member of the National Guard and Army Reserve. Scott was a lawyer at a private practice from 1973 to 1991.

Bob Taft (politician)

Robert Alphonso "Bob" Taft III (born January 8, 1942) is an Ohio Republican Party politician. He was elected to two terms of office as the 67th Governor of the U.S. state of Ohio between 1999 and 2007. After leaving office, Taft started working for the University of Dayton beginning August 15, 2007.

Taft was born in 1942 in Boston, Massachusetts, to U.S. Senator Robert Alphonso Taft, Jr. and Blanca Duncan Noel. Bob's paternal grandfather was U.S. Senate Majority Leader Robert Alphonso Taft, Sr., his patrilineal great-grandfather was U.S. President and U.S. Supreme Court Chief Justice William Howard Taft, and his patrilineal great-great-grandfather was Attorney General and Secretary of War Alphonso Taft.

He was raised in Cincinnati, Ohio, where he attended the Cincinnati Country Day School through the ninth grade and graduated from The Taft School. He attended Yale University, where he was a member of the Yale Political Union, and graduated with a B.A. in government in 1963. From 1963 to 1965, he served as a Peace Corpsvolunteer, teaching in the African nation of Tanzania. He later attended the Woodrow Wilson School of Public and International Affairs at Princeton University, receiving an M.A., again in government, in 1967. In 1976, he received his Juris Doctor from the University of Cincinnati College of Law.

Chapter 8- Bob in History

Bob Wise (poitician)

Robert "Bob" Ellsworth Wise Jr., Congressman and Govenor of West Virgina, was born on January 6, 1948. He was raised in the Kanawha Valley of Kanawha County, West Virginia with his two sisters and attended George Washington High School in nearby Charleston, West Virginia. His father worked in insurance, for McDonough Caperton Group, for thirty years. Wise ran track and field in high school – the half-mile and mile – and was elected vice president of the student body. Wise has won every election he's been in since then.

Wise enrolled at Duke University in 1966, graduating with a Bachelor of Arts in Political Science four years later. After leaving Duke, Wise applied to law school, working as an aide in a California mental health facility until he was accepted at the University of Houston. Wise relocated to Texas for his studies, eventually transferring to the Tulane University School of Law. He waited tables in New Orleans, working nightshifts while he obtained his Juris Doctor.

Wise graduated from Tulane in 1975 and opened his first law practice in Charleston. In his early days as a lawyer Wise helped create West Virginians for a Fair and Equitable Assessment of Taxes (FEAT), a group interested in property tax reform. Wise also advocated for coal miners seeking workers compensation and supported community renewal efforts for the 1972 Buffalo Creek disaster victims. In 1978, he once more helped with redevelopment issues for those affected by the Mingo CountyFloods written in the Scots language, although much of his writing is also in English and a light Scots dialect, accessible to an audience beyond Scotland. He also wrote in standard English, and in these writings his political or civil commentary is often at its bluntest.

Chapter 9

Bob as Artist, Poet, Writer

Chapter 9- Bob as Artist, Writer and Poet

Robert Browning (poet)

settings, and challenging vocabulary and syntax. The speakers in his poems are often musicians or painters whose work functions as a metaphor for poetry.

Browning's early career began promisingly, but was not a success. The long poem *Pauline* brought him to the attention of Dante Gabriel Rossetti, and was followed by *Paracelsus*, which was praised by Wordsworth and Dickens, but in 1840 the difficult *Sordello*, which was seen as wilfully obscure, brought his poetry into disrepute. His reputation took more than a decade to recover, during which time he moved away from the Shelleyan forms of his early period and developed a more personal style.v

Browning's early career began promisingly, but was not a success. The long poem *Pauline* brought him to the attention of Dante Gabriel Rossetti, and was followed by *Paracelsus*, which was praised by Wordsworth and Dickens, but in 1840 the difficult *Sordello*, which was seen as wilfully obscure, brought his poetry into disrepute. His reputation took more than a decade to recover, during which time he moved away from the Shelleyan forms of his early period and developed a more personal style.

In 1846 Browning married the older poet Elizabeth Barrett, who at the time was considerably better known than himself. So started one of history's most famous literary marriages. They went to live in Italy, a country he called 'my university,' and which features frequently in his work. By the time of her death in 1861, he had published the crucial collection *Men and Women*. The collection *Dramatis Personae* and the book-length epic poem *The Ring and the Book* followed, and made him a leading British poet. He continued to write prolifically, but today it is largely the poetry he had written in this middle period on which his reputation rests.

Robert Leslie Conly

(January 11, 1918 – March 5, 1973) (better known by his pen name, Robert C. O'Brien) was an American author and journalist for*National Geographic Magazine*. Conly was the third of five children from a wealthy Irish-Catholic family. With interests in music and literature, Conly entered Williams College in 1935 but left in his second year. He then went through a period that he referred to as his "breakdown", briefly working in Albany, New York before going back to his family in disgrace. Although he later studied for a time at Juilliard, he went on to receive his Bachelor of Arts in English at the University of Rochester in 1940.

Chapter 9- Bob as Artist, Writer and Poet

Robert Ferro (writer)

(October 21, 1941 - July 11, 1988) was an American novelist whose semi-autobiographical fiction explored the uneasy integration of homosexuality and traditional American upper-middle-class values.

He was born in Cranford, New Jersey. He went to college at Rutgers University and received a Master's Degree from theUniversity of Iowa. In the fall of 1965 Ferro met Andrew Holleran at the Iowa Writer's Workshop. He later lectured atAdelphi University. He was a member of The Violet Quill.
He died of AIDS a few months after his partner, Michael Grumley, in 1988 at his father's home in Ho-Ho-Kus, New Jersey, age 46. Following their deaths, the Ferro-Grumley Foundation, which manages their estate, created and endowed the annual Ferro-Grumley Award for LGBT fiction in conjunction with Publishing Triangle.

Robert Frost (poet)

(March 26, 1874 – January 29, 1963) was an American poet. His work was initially published in England before it was published in America. He is highly regarded for his realistic depictions of rural life and his command of American colloquial speech. His work frequently employed settings from rural life in New England in the early twentieth century, using them to examine complex social and philosophical themes. One of the most popular and critically respected American poets of the twentieth century, Frost was honored frequently during his lifetime, receiving four Pulitzer Prizes for Poetry. He became one of America's rare "public literary figures, almost an artistic institution." [1] He was awarded the Congressional Gold Medal in 1960 for his poetical works. On July 22, 1961, Frost was named Poet laureate of Vermont.

Robert Dennis Harris (writer)

Born March 7, 1957, he is an English novelist. He is a former journalist and television reporter. Although he began his career in non-fiction, his fame rests upon his works of historical fiction. Beginning with the best-seller *Fatherland*, Harris focused on surrounding the Second World War, followed by works set in ancient Rome. His most recent works centre on contemporary history.

Robert A. Heinlein (writer)

(July 7, 1907 – May 8, 1988) was an American science fiction writer. Often called the "dean of science fiction writers", he was an influential and controversial author of the genre in his time.He was one of the first science fiction writers to break into mainstream magazines such as *The Saturday Evening Post* in the late 1940s. He was one of the best-selling science fiction novelists for many decades, and he, Isaac Asimov, and Arthur C. Clarke are often considered to be the "Big Three" of science fiction authors.

A notable writer of science fiction short stories, Heinlein was one of a group of writers who came to prominence under the editorship of John W. Campbell, Jr. in his *Astounding Science Fiction* magazine—though Heinlein denied that Campbell influenced his writing to any great degree.Within the framework of his science fiction stories, Heinlein repeatedly addressed certain social themes: the importance of individual liberty and self-reliance, the obligation individuals owe to their societies, the influence of organized religion on culture and government, and the tendency of society to repress nonconformist thought. He also speculated on the influence of space travel on human cultural practices.

Robert Ludlum,

(May 25, 1927 – March 12, 2001) was an American author of 27 thriller novels. The number of copies of his books in print is estimated between 290 million and 500 million. They have been published in 33 languages and 40 countries. Ludlum also published books under the pseudonyms **Jonathan Ryder** and **Michael Shepherd.**[5] (May

Many of Ludlum's novels have been made into films and mini-series, including *The Osterman Weekend, The Holcroft Covenant, The Apocalypse Watch, The Bourne Identity, The Bourne Supremacy* and *The Bourne Ultimatum. Covert One: The Hades Factor*, a book co-written with Gayle Lynds, was originally conceived as a mini-series; the book evolved from a short treatment Ludlum wrote for NBC. The Bourne movies, starring Matt Damon in the title role, have been commercially and critically successful (*The Bourne Ultimatum* won three Academy Awards in 2008), although the story lines depart significantly from the source material.

Chapter 9- Bob as Artist, Writer and Poet

Robert Motherwell (artist)

Robert "Bob" Motherwell was born in Aberdeen, Washington on January 24, 1915, the first child of Robert Burns Motherwell II and Margaret Hogan Motherwell. The family later moved to San Francisco, where Motherwell's father served as president of Wells Fargo Bank. Due to the artist's asthmatic condition, Motherwell was reared largely on the Pacific Coast and spent most of his school years in California. There he developed a love for the broad spaces and bright colours that later emerged as essential characteristics of his abstract paintings (ultramarine blue of the sky and ochre yellow of Californian hills). His later concern with themes of mortality can likewise be traced to his frail health as a child.
Between 1932 and 1937, Motherwell briefly studied painting at California School of Fine Arts, San Francisco and received a BA in philosophy from Stanford University. At Stanford Motherwell was introduced to modernism through his extensive reading of symbolist and other literature, especially Mallarmé, James Joyce, Edgar Allan Poe, and Octavio Paz. This passion stayed with Motherwell for the rest of his life and became a major theme of his later paintings and drawings.

Robert Rauschenberg (artist)

Robert "Bob" Rauschenberg (October 22, 1925 – May 12, 2008) was an American painter and graphic artist whose early works anticipated the pop art movement. Rauschenberg is well known for his "Combines" of the 1950s, in which non-traditional materials and objects were employed in innovative combinations. Rauschenberg was both a painter and a sculptor and the Combines are a combination of both, but he also worked with photography, printmaking, papermaking, and performance. He was awarded the National Medal of Arts in 1993. He became the recipient of the Leonardo da Vinci World Award of Arts in 1995 in recognition of his more than 40 years of fruitful artmaking.

Rauschenberg lived and worked in New York City as well as on Captiva Island, Florida until his death from heart failure on May 12, 2008.

Rauschenberg was born as Milton Ernest Rauschenberg in Port Arthur, Texas, the son of Dora Carolina (née Matson) and Ernest R. Rauschenberg. His father was of German and Cherokee ancestry and his mother of Anglo-Saxon descent. His parents were Fundamentalist Christians. Rauschenberg was afflicted withdyslexia. At 16, Rauschenberg was admitted to the University of Texas where he began studying pharmacy. He was drafted into the United States Navy in 1943. Based in California, he served as a mental hospital technician until his discharge in 1945. Rauschenberg subsequently studied at the Kansas City Art Institute and the Académie Julian in Paris, France, where he met the painter Susan Weil. In 1948 Rauschenberg and Weil decided to attend Black Mountain College in North Carolina.

Josef Albers, a founder of the Bauhaus, became Rauschenberg's painting instructor at Black Mountain. Albers' preliminary courses relied on strict discipline that did not allow for any "uninfluenced experimentation". Rauschenberg described Albers as influencing him to do "exactly the reverse" of what he was being taught.

From 1949 to 1952 Rauschenberg studied with Vaclav Vytlacil and Morris Kantor at the Art Students League of New York, where he met fellow artists Knox Martin and Cy Twombly.

Bob Ross (artist)

Robert Norman "Bob" Ross (October 29, 1942 – July 4, 1995) was an American painter, art instructor, and television host. He was best known as the creator and host of The Joy of Painting, a television program that aired on PBS in the United States, Canada, and Europe.

Bob Ross was born on October 29, 1942 in Daytona Beach, Florida. Ross was raised in Orlando, Florida. Ross had a half brother Jim, whom he mentioned in passing on his show.

While working as a carpenter with his father, Ross lost part of his left index finger. It did not affect the way he held his palette while painting.

Robert Kimmel Smith (writer)

Born July 31, 1930, Brooklyn, New York Smith is a novelist and award-winning American children's author. Between 1957 and 1965, he was a copywriter at an ad agency, and was a partner and creative director at Smith and Toback from 1967 to 1970. In 1970 he became a full-time writer; his first children's book, *Chocolate Fever*, was published in 1972. As of 1996, *Chocolate Fever* had sold nearly 2 million paperback copies and was listed at number 92 on *Publishers Weekly*'s all-time list of bestselling children's paperbacks. His other works for young readers include *Jelly Belly* and *The War with Grandpa.*

Robert Penn Warren (poet)
(April 24, 1905 – September 15, 1989) was an American poet, novelist, and literary critic and was one of the founders of New Criticism. He was also a charter member of the Fellowship of Southern Writers. He founded the influential literary journal *The Southern Review* with Cleanth Brooks in 1935. He received the Pulitzer Prize in 1947 for his novel *All the King's Men* (1946) and the Pulitzer Prize for Poetry in 1958 and 1979. He is the only person to have won Pulitzer Prizes for both fiction and poetry. Warren's best-known

work is *All the King's Men*, a novel that won the Pulitzer Prize in 1947. Main character Willie Starkresembles Huey Pierce Long (1893–1935), the radical populist governor of Louisiana whom Warren was able to observe closely while teaching at Louisiana State University in Baton Rouge from 1933 to 1942. *All the King's Men* became a highly successful film, starring Broderick Crawford and winning the Academy Award for Best Picture in 1949. A 2006 film adaptation by writer/director Steven Zaillian featured Sean Penn as Willie Stark and Jude Law as Jack Burden. The opera *Willie Stark* by Carlisle Floyd to his own libretto based on the novel was premiered in 1981.

Warren served as the Consultant in Poetry to the Library of Congress, 1944–1945 (later termed Poet Laureate), and won two Pulitzer Prizes in poetry, in 1958 for *Promises: Poems 1954–1956* and in 1979 for *Now and Then. Promises* also won the annual National Book Award for Poetry. In 1974, the National Endowment for the Humanities selected him for the Jefferson Lecture, the U.S. federal government's highest honor for achievement in the humanities. Warren's lecture was entitled "Poetry and Democracy" (subsequently published under the title *Democracy and Poetry*). In 1980, Warren was presented with the Presidential Medal of Freedom by President Jimmy Carter. In 1981, Warren was selected as a MacArthur Fellow and later was named as the first U.S. Poet Laureate Consultant in Poetry on February 26, 1986. In 1987, he was awarded the National Medal of Arts.

Bob Woodward (journalist)

Robert Upshur "Bob" Woodward (born March 26, 1943) is an American investigative and non-fiction author. He has worked for *The Washington Post* since 1971 as a reporter, and is now an associate editor of the *Post*.
While a young reporter for *The Washington Post* in 1972, Woodward was teamed up with Carl Bernstein; the two did much of the original news reporting on the Watergate scandal. These scandals led to numerous government investigations and the eventual resignation of President Richard Nixon. Gene Roberts, the former executive editor of *The Philadelphia Inquirer* and former managing editor of *The New York Times*, has called the work of Woodward and Bernstein "maybe the single greatest reporting effort of all time".

Woodward continued to work for *The Washington Post* after his reporting on Watergate. He has since written 16 books on American politics, 12 of which have been bestsellers. Woodward made crucial contributions to two Pulitzer Prizes won by *The Washington Post*. First he and Bernstein were the lead reporters on Watergate and the *Post* won the Pulitzer Prize for Public Service in 1973. He was also the main reporter for the *Post*'s Coverage of the September 11 attacks in 2001. The *Post* won the 2002 Pulitzer Prize for National Reporting for ten of its stories on the subject.

Chapter 9- Bob as Artist, Writer and Poet

Woodward himself has been a recipient of nearly every major American journalism award, including the Heywood Brounaward (1972), Worth Bingham Prize for Investigative Reporting (1972 and 1986), Sigma Delta Chi Award (1973), George Polk Award (1972), William Allen White Medal (2000), and the Gerald R. Ford Prize for Reporting on the Presidency (2002). In 2012, Colby College presented Woodward with the Elijah Parish Lovejoy Award for courageous journalism as well as an honorary doctorate.

Woodward has authored or co-authored 16 nonfiction books in the last 35 years. All 16 have been national bestsellers and 12 of them have been No. 1 national nonfiction bestsellers—more No. 1 national nonfiction bestsellers than any contemporary author. He has written multiple No. 1 national nonfiction bestsellers on a wide range of subjects in each of the four decades he has been active as an author, from 1974 to 2009.

In his 1995 memoir, *A Good Life,* former *Post* executive editor Ben Bradlee singled out Woodward in the foreword. "It would be hard to overestimate the contributions to my newspaper and to my time as editor of that extraordinary reporter, Bob Woodward—surely the best of his generation at investigative reporting, the best I've ever seen.... And Woodward has maintained the same position on top of journalism's ladder ever since Watergate."
David Gergen, who had worked in the White House during the Richard Nixon and three subsequent administrations, said in his 2000 memoir, *Eyewitness to Power*, of Woodward's reporting, "I don't accept everything he writes as gospel—he can get details wrong—but generally, his accounts in both his books and in the Post are remarkably reliable and demand serious attention. I am convinced he writes only what he believes to be true or has been reliably told to be true. And he is certainly a force for keeping the government honest."
Fred Barnes of the *Weekly Standard* called Woodward "the best pure reporter of his generation, perhaps ever." In 2003, Albert Hunt of *The Wall Street Journal* called Woodward "the most celebrated journalist of our age." In 2004, Bob Schiefferof CBS News said, "Woodward has established himself as the best reporter of our time. He may be the best reporter of all time."

Chapter 10

Quotations from BOB

Chapter 10- Quotations from Bob

The truth is everyone is going to hurt you.
You just got to go to find the ones worth suffering for.

Bob Marley

Let's release the lobster back into the supermarket from whence it came.

Bob's Burgers

All I can do is be me, whoever that is.

Bob Dylan

Health food may be good for the conscience but Oreos taste a hell of a lot better.

Robert Redford

Something is wrong with America. I wonder sometimes what people are thinking about or if they're thinking at all.

Bob Dole

You learned the two greatest thing in life, never rat on your friends, and always keep your mouth shut.

Robert De Niro

Chapter 10- Quotations from Bob

Right now, I'm worth a million dollars, and I owe Uncle Sam a million-and-a-half dollars, and I made a deal with him. I said, 'Uncle Sam, I'm going to pay you 25 grand a month.'

Robert Blake

Go vegetable heavy. Reverse the psychology of your plate by making meat the side dish and vegetables the main course.

Bobby Flay

You know you're getting old when the candles cost more than the cake.

Bob Hope

Gilligan's Island is wherever you want it to be in your mind.

Bob Denver

There are those who look at things the way they are, and ask why... I dream of things that never were, and ask why not?

Bobby Kennedy

Soon, I'm going to meet somebody around my own age, and she's going to be smart and beautiful, and I'm going to date her daughter.

Bob Saget

I was the fattest baby in Clark County, Arkansas. They put me in the newspaper. It was like a prize turnip.

Billy Bob Thornton

I don't like country music, but I don't mean to denigrate those who do. And for the people who like country music, denigrate means 'put down'.

Bob Newhart

I can tell you that I'd rather be kissed by my dogs than by some people I've known.

Bob Barker

One of the big secrets of finding time is not to watch television.

Bob Keeshan (Captain Kangaroo)

Love is when two people who care for each other get confused.

Bob Schneider

You can't trust politicians. It doesn't matter who makes a political speech. It's all lies - and it applies to any rock star who wants to make a political speech as well.

Bob Geldof

Buildings designed exclusively on scientific principles will depress their occupants and constrain their creativity.

Robert Evans

You can’t kid a kid. They know right away if you like them or not.

Buffalo Bob Smith

Chapter 10- Quotations from Bob

Movies bore me; especially my own. I've still got the same attitude I had when I started. I haven't changed anything but my underwear.

Robert Mitchum

Never answer the question that has been asked of you. Answer the question you wish had been asked of you.

Robert McNamara

Watergate provides a model case study of the interaction and powers of each of the branches of government. It also is a morality play with a sad and dramatic ending.

Bob Woodward

Poetry is when an emotion has found its thought and the thought has found words.

Robert Frost

Every professional athlete owes a debt of gratitude to the fans and management, and pays an installment every time he plays. He should never miss a payment.

Bobby Hull

Unfortunately, a lot of people are stupid. They take drugs. They get drunk and do all the wrong things in life. I just played it straight.

Bobby Vinton

Baseball hasn't forgotten me. I go to a lot of old-timers games and I haven't lost a thing. I sit in the bullpen and let people throw things at me. Just like old times.

Bob Uecker

Chapter 10- Quotations from Bob

Who am I that I have to sing under an umbrella? These people are my fans, and if they can stand in the rain to hear me sing, I can stand in the rain.

Bobby Darin

Do your best when no one is looking. If you do that, then you can be successful in anything that you put your mind to.

Bob Cousy

I'm not gonna need my toys any more. After I learn Sex Ed, I'll be too busy dating.

Bobby Hill (King of the Hill)

You can accomplish anything you want if you act like you've already accomplished it.

Bob Cummings

Yeah. And the thing is, it was only a few years ago that I got a good credit rating because I had IRS liens against property.

Bobby Braddock

Most painting in the European tradition was painting the mask. Modern art rejected all that. Our subject matter was the person behind the mask.

Robert Motherwell

I've played so many historical characters because most horrible dictators are short, fat, middle-aged men.

Bob Hoskins

Chapter 11

Unlikely Quotations never said about BOB

Chapter 11 - Unlikely Quotations Never Said About BOB

And a BOB shall lead them.

The Good, the Bad and the BOBs.

Is this a BOB I see before me?

Out, out, damn BOB!

To BOB or not to BOB? That is the question.

Hey look. It's the BOB twins, BOB and BOB.

A BOB in the hand is worth two in the bush.

You bet your BOB!

That's BOBsome!

He's just BOBalicious!

I feel a BOB coming on.

Send me your tired, your weak, your BOBs.

Chapter 11 - Unlikely Quotations Never Said About BOB

A BOB in time saves nine.

BOB, build me an ark.

Give me liberty, or give me BOB.

It does not matter how slowly you go, as long as you do not BOB.

Got BOB?

Ask not what BOB can do for your country.
Ask what your country can do for BOB.

Oh Danny BOB.

We’re gonna need a bigger BOB.

BOB Ahoy!

BOB goes the weasel!

I’m BOBBING in the rain, just BOBBING in the rain.

BOB’s your aunt!

Chapter 11 - Unlikely Quotations Never Said About BOB

Now that's what I call a BOB.

A BOB in every pot!

A BOB off the old block.

Excuse me, do you have a BOB?

You can bet your BOB on it!

May the BOB be with you.

You call that a BOB?

BOBBY, the Red-Nosed Reindeer.

Not my cup of BOB.

Bring your own Bob.

Go ye forth and BOB.

I've seen some BOB's, but this BOB takes the cake?

Chapter 11 - Unlikely Quotations Never Said About BOB

From BOB to Eternity.

Bob, the Eagle has landed.

Excuse me waiter, there's a Bob in my soup.

That guy is such a Bob!

Many are called, but only Bob is chosen.

You wanna Bob? I'll give you a Bob!

Well, as Bob always said…

Once a Bob, always a Bob.

Other publications by Robert John "Bob" Keiber

available on Amazon.com and other online vendors and bookstores.

Fear Is Good, A Survival Guide for Public Speaking.

Urban Hykool, Haiku Poetry About New York City

My Cancer Diary, Inspiration Journal for Cancer Patients

For bulk orders or author book signings and presentations

Contact: **The Tuxedo Group**- 212-252-2065

Sources for biographical material; Wikipedia.com

Sources for quoted material; Brainy Quotes.com

If there are other Bobs you would like to have included in Vol. 2, please send your suggestions to the publisher, or go to Facebook's BOOK OF BOB page, "like"and comment your suggestion.

May The BOB Be With You.

Notes:

www.ingramcontent.com/pod-product-compliance
Lightning Source LLC
Chambersburg PA
CBHW070426290526
45791CB00005B/1856

* 9 7 8 1 5 1 5 0 8 3 2 5 2 *